Dog's Best Friend

DOG'S BEST FRIEND

Journey to the Roots of an Ancient Partnership

Ursula Birr
Gerald Krakauer
Daniela Osiander

Park Street Press
Rochester, Vermont

Park Street Press
One Park Street
Rochester, Vermont 05767
www.InnerTraditions.com

Park Street Press is a division of Inner Traditions International

Library of Congress Cataloging-in-Publication Data

Birr, Ursula.
    [Abenteur Hund. English]
    Dog's best friend : journey to the roots of an ancient partnership /
Ursula Birr, Gerald Krakauer, Daniela Osiander.
        p.   cm.
    ISBN 0-89281-829-8 (alk. paper)
    1. Dogs. 2. Human-animal relationships. 3. Dogs—Pictorial works.
I. Krakauer, Gerald. II. Osiander, Daniela, 1966– . III. Title.
SF426.2.B5813   1999
636.7'009—dc21   99-14170
                                                            CIP

Printed and bound in Hong Kong

10 9 8 7 6 5 4 3 2 1

Text design and layout by Kristin Camp
This book was typeset in Goudy and Stone Sans

CONTENTS

GREENLAND
Companions in Ice and Snow   62

NAMIBIA
The Dogs of the Red Herders   84

NEPAL
On the Tracks of the Holy Dogs   100

MOROCCO
Kitmir's Heirs   118

Preface

This book is based on a television series that we worked on for almost four years. The idea behind it is much older. It was conceived in 1986 at the World Congress of the Delta Society held in Boston. There, scientists from around the world debated the relationship between humans and animals. We heard and learned a lot, but one thought in particular fascinated us: that it would be incredibly exciting to trace back to its origin the oldest animal-man relationship. To even begin to realize this project, we had to travel to faraway countries and visit foreign cultures. Our travels involved visiting people who to this day live in a mutually dependant relationship with their dogs, people whose traditions, culture, and way of life remain largely untouched by the influences of industrialized civilization. We brought together the many encounters and experiences from our travels and present them in this book. It was not completely unexpected that it grew beyond a single chapter about the history of dogs into a comprehensive look at the development of human social behavior that—among hunters, gatherers, and herdsmen—is in many ways characterized by the ties between humans and dogs. Because of the latest and sometimes dramatic developments in the living space of humans, there is reason to be concerned that much of what we were able to see, experience, and document will soon cease to exist. Because of this, *Dog's Best Friend* has unintentionally also become a voyage into the past of humankind.

Introduction

It is likely that no other animal has influenced humans' social development in as long lasting a way as the dog. During the more than fourteen thousand years that dogs and humans have been in contact, the dog has been companion, protector, and helper. "He is the sanctuary of the tired, model of faithfulness, mirror image of attention, pearl of understanding and memory, motto and mascot of the wise," wrote the historian Christian Franz Pollini

The TV crew of Pro Sieben: cameraman Walter Franke, producer Gerald Krakauer, and author Daniela Osiander in a river taxi on their way to the middle of Borneo.

about the family of dogs nearly three hundred years ago, a statement that still is true today.

Humans love their dogs and in turn are loved by them. As family pets, dogs are the playmates of children and have great instructional value. When under the care of older people, they are often the last real responsibility in life, and for individuals living alone, dogs are great companions. In a rapidly changing world dogs are often the last link to nature. While in sheer numbers dogs do not rank first among pets, they are undisputedly the most important ones. Recent scientific studies have even proven their therapeutic usefulness: if one pats a dog, the pulse slows and blood pressure drops. Those who live with dogs experience more rapid recovery after illness. The daily walks that dogs demand keep people fit and also encourage contact with the outside world.

But what are the roots for this modern partnership? What was it like, the first cohabitation of Stone Age humans and their wolflike animals? Many scientists, such as Austrian Nobel laureate Konrad Lorenz, have tried to shed light on the hazy history of the original dog. In his 1949 book *Man Meets Dog* Lorenz sketched out the ancient partnership:

During filming of the TV series one thing was consistent with all the four-legged main actors: to make them understand the set directions, they all had to be bribed in a loving way.

Through the tall grass of the plain a small group of men creeps along, simple pieces of animal skin covering their genitals. They carry spears as well as blades and arrows made from bones. Two carry the left-overs of a wild boar, originally the prize of a tiger they had come upon during his meal and prompted to retreat with their wild screams. The destination of the group is a cave at the edge of the desert where women and children already hungrily await their re-turn. While the meat is roasted over the campfire, sounds from the plain can be heard in the cave. They are made by jackals, who have followed the group throughout the day. One of the men takes a piece of the roasted meat and throws it in the direction of the sounds. Maybe he is trying to entice the jackals to come closer to the fire, since they announce any approaching animal well in advance.

Whether the beginnings of this ancient partnership were actually simi-lar or different to this is open to speculation. But what we do know today is that the domesticated dog descended not from the jackal but from the wolf. We can also speculate that it must have been puppies who were originally taken into a community of humans. Perhaps families came upon them while gathering berries, fruits, insects, and frogs, and—if they did not eat them—they might have reared them. Stone Age humans quickly recognized the usefulness of these dogs. Their adaptable nature allowed them to become guards, housemates, children's playmates, and eaters of leftovers. They assisted with transportation and later with hunting. When humans worked in unison with the dog, even the harshest of climates suddenly became manageable. Hunters in Greenland and herdsmen in Africa continue to use the advantage of this partnership today as did all of our ancestors.

To go from use to abuse takes only a small step. Yet none of the peoples we met on our travels who keep dogs have taken this step. It is as though the biblical wisdom of King Solomon turned into law: "He who is just knows the needs of his animals, but the heart of the wanton is hard."

The seven chapters that follow tell of the many who are just and of their animals. And to their dogs we want to leave a memorial: without them we quite possibly never would have left the Stone Age.

BURKINA FASO

Greyhounds in the Desert Sand

If the master is aggressive,
his dog will not be peaceful.
<small>PROVERB OF THE KEL EWEY-TUAREG</small>

In the heat of the day the young female dog passed huts and hedges with a relaxed gait even as her swollen body weighed heavily on her long legs. Everyone could see Taikoussou lying down in the yellow-red dust at the middle of the village square. It was here in full view of the settlement that she felt assured of the community's protection.

Taikoussou was about to give birth for the first time. A little later she would do so without fuss and with the great calm for which the mothers of this race have been renowned for the past five hundred generations. "Taikou, loussou!" She heard the gentle words of her master who knelt down in the sand beside her. Ayad ak Inschanan's voice had the same soft tone he had used at the birth of each one of his eleven children, born by his two wives behind a partition in his hut.

Ayad and his family were the only ones who call the animal by her proper name and, therefore, they had a special relationship with her. The other villagers called her Takhchit, which in the language of the Tuareg means something akin to "the electrified." In their interactions with the greyhounds many of the other peoples of the Sahel use the language of the original masters of this dog race. Even if the dogs among them are mainly kept—as they were with Ayad from the tribe of the Fulbe-Peul—because of their beauty and as guards for the herds, they originally were bred as hunting companions for the riding nomads of the north: the Tuareg.

Azawakh, the name that Western dog lovers have given them, was derived from the Wadi Asuak, a valley in the middle Niger basin. Three West African states share the area over which these dogs are currently spread: Mali, Niger, and Burkina Faso, the former Upper Volta. Here, close to a border garrison in Mali, we meet Ayad, his family, and his Taikoussou.

A sigh emerged from deep down in the dog's throat, a sound like the rough growling of a large turtle in the reeds of the Beli, the river that marks

6

the border to Mali. Then a shiny, round body emerged from between the hind legs of the animal—Taikoussou's first puppy. She licked it off and opened the placenta, which she ate. She then nudged the puppy, which was smaller than even the narrow head of its mother, toward her stomach and nipples. This process was repeated five more times, and after two hours had passed Taikoussou had given birth to six puppies.

Taikoussou has become a mother for the first time, giving birth to six healthy puppies without any help from her master.

Idi or *eidi* (plural: *iadan*) is what the race is called in the language of the southern Sahel. Northern Tuareg tribes in Algeria call the dogs *oska*, which generally means the "hunting greyhound," but refers mostly to the *sloughi*, which in the past has often been mistaken as the azawakh by Europeans. The dog is best characterized by the name given to it in the language of the Tuareg: *idi n'illeli*, the "greyhound of the free nomads."

This race of dogs first served as hunting companions of the independent riding tribes of the desert and as the guards of their nomadic herds. For thousands of years these dogs have fulfilled these expectations perfectly and they continue to do so in the constantly shrinking territories and incessantly worsening conditions for both humans and dogs. Where once upon a time hunters had valuable game in gazelles, antelopes, and sheep, today their needs must be satisfied with rabbits and lizards. For humans as well as for dogs, the only thing remaining of the hunt is the ritual.

Burkina Faso

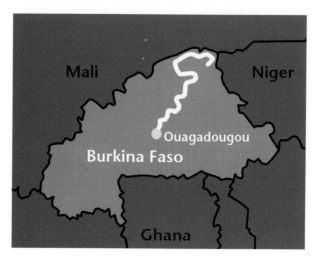

The northern part of the West African inland state Burkina Faso belongs to the Sahel. The Arabic word Sahel (shore) refers to the belt two to three hundred kilometers wide that stretches south of the Sahara across the continent from the Atlantic Ocean to the Horn of Africa. Its northern and southern borders are characterized by rolling hills. For centuries the Sahel was the economic and cultural link and area of contact between the Arabic Berber people of the north and the black African population of the south. It was the final destination of many caravan routes from both directions and the meeting point of the Islamic-Arabic and black African animistic religions. The once rich and powerful region is today characterized by poverty and growing destruction. On one hand, the causes for this are the recurring natural catastrophes such as droughts that bring about water and food scarcity, a high infant mortality rate, and epidemics, and on the other hand the destruction of natural resources made worse by humans through deforestation, overgrazing, and expansion of farmland.

These circumstances, which already create terrible suffering, are exacerbated by the political developments in the greater area of North Africa, which especially victimize marginal peoples and tribes such as the Tuareg. Materially the Sahel states are among the poorest countries of the world; and the poorest among their population are often the once free masters of the desert, the Tuareg. However, the victims also include their dogs—the azawakhs.

So far very little has changed in the living arrangements and nothing has changed in the measure of respect between humans and dogs here, 450 kilometers from Ouagadougou, the capital of Burkina Faso. Ayad, a sedentary cattle farmer and oasis builder, demonstrates this to us. Not once does he have to lend a helping hand, but like a guard kneels

next to the dog throughout the entire birth process. Only after the labor is complete does he show his joy and curiosity. In a clear sign of her devotion, Taikoussou lets him look at her puppies—human and dog completely trusting each other. Ayad immediately establishes that the puppies are strong and healthy, and is especially interested in their color and sex. Ayad smiles. Pride of the breeder? Pride of a father? It is hard to tell.

But pride is most certainly involved because a litter of good dogs, preferably males, brings honor to its owner. This goes for the Fulbe as well as for the Tuareg, for the sedentary as well as for the nomad. Even though both peoples adhere to Islam, which differentiates animals based on their purity, it seems as though here, in the harsh conditions of the semidesert in the thornbush and dry savannas, the more strictly interpreted rules of Muhammad have been adjusted to a way of life understands utility as its prime objective. While Muslims in cities and villages may consider dogs to be as filthy as pigs, here in the country the greyhounds, the iadan, are worthy companions of nobility.

It is the conditions of the Sahara, the *bahr bela ma*, the sea without water, and that of the Sahel, the "shore" of this sea, that has caused this adaptation of religious and social norms. This is how camels, horses, and these dogs came to be valued helpers. This is made especially clear by the customs and beliefs of the Tuareg who are convinced that animals, especially those with whom they are in contact, are much like themselves in nature and spirit. Animals can experience happiness and have friends, develop social relations

The dogs are allowed to move freely around the settlement. They guard the campsite and the cattle. Nobody here would think of tying up these noble animals; the people say that the soul of a greyhound wants to roam.

The dog is an important part of the millennia-old Tuareg culture. It was bred primarily for the hunt and as a protecting companion for the caravans.

Like all greyhounds the azawakhs only start participating in the hunt once the hunters have stirred up the game. Where once gazelles and antelopes promised a rich prey, people and dogs now have to be satisfied with rabbits.

or the need to act independently. They are always considered as individuals. When the life of a goat ends here under the butcher's knife, it has been spared up to that point any cruelty born of indifference.

Characteristic of this position is the response of a nomad cattle farmer to the question of why he chose to move on with his herd even though their camp would still provide enough plants for grazing. The Targi (singular of Tuareg) explains it like this to the foreigner: "You wouldn't be happy either about a bowl out of which somebody else has already eaten. The same goes for the goats. They don't respect a shrub on which another goat has gnawed already. If we were to stay here the animals would eat without joy or appetite."

Herdsman philosophy to be sure, but behind it stands a culture that probably originated here in the inland of northwest Africa more than eight thousand years ago. Rock paintings confirm this: they document, up to the first centuries after Christ, the rise and fall of great kingdoms and the wanderings of many tribes and peoples, as well as the importance of animals in these states and empires. The birth of their culture was made possible by horses and camels, but dogs too belonged with them for protection.

In 1607 the Arabic Andalusian geographer El Bekri reported on the

The Tuareg

Once upon a time the Tuareg were one of the most independent and free tribes of the Sahara and the Sahel. About five hundred thousand people of their tribe still live in the central Sahara, in Niger, Mali, Burkina Faso, Algeria, and Libya. They are nomadic hunters, but also cattle farmers (goats, sheep, and camels—the last only for the noble caste).

The structure of their society, which has been strongly influenced by Islam, resembles a pyramid. At the top are the aristocratic warriors, the nobility, the free, who are called Imascheren. Beneath them is the caste of the Ineslemen, those who know how to write—teachers and priests. This group is followed by the vassals (Imrad), goat keepers and herdsmen who all have to pay tribute to the nobility. Among larger tribes the Iklan belong to this caste; they are slaves, mostly descendants of black Africans.

There are many different Tuareg tribes that travel throughout the greater area of northwest Africa. Because of Africa's decolonization and also because of recent religious-fundamentalist and political-nationalist currents, the Tuareg have been harassed by all the governments of these states. In Algeria the Tuareg are persecuted and scorned because they sided with the French in Algeria's war for independence. The promise of their own state made by the French was never realized. In Mali the army, until recently, was waging a bitter war against the insubordinate herder warriors: Niger and Libya have restricted the possibility of the Tuareg using areas for grazing; and because of its location in the Sahel, Burkina Faso can in the long run only offer the Tuareg a sedentary lifestyle (although Burkina Faso at least allows the culture of the Tuareg, which Algeria and Mali are bitterly trying to eradicate). Regardless, in the end this forced change from a nomadic to a sedentary lifestyle will still bring about the destruction of this culture.

White camels, the men's blue facecloths, and long swords and round shields of this tribe caused the early European explorers to call these best known of the Saharan people the "blue knights of the desert." They have been known since Roman times, when they were called Garamants. Today's name, Tuareg, comes from the Arabic word Targa, which is the name of the Libyan oasis region of Fezzan, where once the Garamant capital Garama was located.

To this day dogs live closely with the families of the Tuareg. The harsh living conditions of the desert forced the nomads to make a strict selection. Only the strongest and most beautiful animals were allowed to live.

court of the king of Ghana, a monarchy that occupied the area of today's Mauritania and Mali. At lavish receptions, horses wearing golden jewelry would surround the king in his tent. The entrance to the tent was guarded by dogs who would never leave the monarch's side. To signify their high rank they were decorated with collars made of gold and silver bells.

Empires fell and new ones were founded by conquerors from the north and east. City-states came into existence; Arabic-Islamic and black African animistic cultures began to intermix. Invaders continually formed new states, subduing vassals and amassing mighty armies. Often it was only the long trade routes through the Sahara and Sahel that connected the fighting monarchs, who in spite of their wars continued to trade salt, gold, copper, slaves, and ivory.

A great culture was created, one with many facets and different ways of life and that changed from century to century. And along with the Arabic spirit for inventions and the African expertise with arts and crafts, the countenance of the Saharan and trans-Saharan states of today was shaped by three different animals: the horse, the camel, and the dog.

The first two animals created the routes, but only the dog made the routes safe for travel and helped humans to obtain food on long journeys. In the north and east these dogs must have been the ancestor of today's sloughis; farther to the south it was the idi n'illeli, the azawakh, who in the process of their long and isolated development became a separate and distinct race, and who were unknown to the Western world until just a few decades ago.

The characteristics and build the azawakh has today are attributable to the peoples with whom it lived for the longest time and with whom it has the closest ties: the Tuareg. They made the azawakh agile and fast enough to hunt gazelles and rabbits and courageous enough to drive away hyenas and jackals. They gave the dog the endurance of a camel and the beauty of noble Arabic horses. Not much fuss was made to build these characteristics; they are the result of a strict and, according to Western standards, cruel selection. But the life of the Tuareg, which was constantly endangered by harsh nature and enemies, left them no choice. From a litter of newborn azawakhs only the strongest and most beautiful male survived to become a hunting dog. Occasionally a female was kept for purposes of further procreation. Black puppies were almost always killed since a bad spirit was believed to be inside of them. The other "surplus" puppies had to die as well. An animal chosen to live had to prove its worth.

Survival of the fittest is a principle of nature. With the Tuareg this meant that azawakhs who showed any signs of weakness or did not abide by the strict rules governing the cohabitation of humans and dogs were killed. The result of this rigid selection was a race of dogs truly rare with strength of body and character, dogs equipped with an impressive genetic heritage.

No nomadic tribe of the Tuareg would have brought up a litter of six puppies as Ayad does. Transportation would be too difficult and obtaining food too expensive, and there would have been too many dogs for their purposes. Here, however, in the village of the sedentary Fulbe, the situation is different. With millet porridge, goat intestines, and the occasional lizard caught by the dogs themselves, Taikoussou and her puppies are fed.

There are no transportation problems, and there is a use for the dogs— as protectors of the herds and villages and as a valuable and much appreciated gift for a guest with whom one might want to start a good relationship. There is also another temptation: villagers, even in remote parts of the homeland of the azawakh, have learned, more so than the Tuareg, that their dogs are worth a lot of money to some visitors, sometimes so much money that an entire village can live off the dog's sale for several weeks. However, such trade is, so far, not common practice, but is rather the exception.

It used to be next to impossible for visitors to buy an azawakh. Asking a nomad Tuareg how much he would sell his greyhound for is like asking him how much he would accept for his oldest son. That is why the first

dogs to appear in Europe at the beginning of the 1970s were almost all presents, a noble gesture toward a newfound and respected friend.

The transition of formerly nomadic cattle farmers or hunters to the lifestyle of a sedentary cattle farmers presents the risk of compromising the looks and character of the azawakhs. So far, however, this is only a risk, not a probability.

Manafi gives us an example of how a changing lifestyle does not necessarily affect a Targi's relationship to the greyhounds. This Tuareg nobleman has since his birth lived south of Mali's border in safe Burkina Faso. Here he eventually settled with his wife and seven children to protect his family from the attacks on the Tuareg and to avoid being dragged into the civil–war-like conflicts in Mali and Niger. He too owns azawakhs: for as long as he can remember greyhounds have been a part of his family. The other Tuareg in the small settlement, noblemen as well as their slaves (who have now been freed by the law of republican Burkina), also own iadan.

One surprising thing is that almost all the dogs we saw are strong dogs who,

Only since 1981 has the greyhound of the Tuareg been recognized as an independent race, the azawakh. The name comes from a valley in the lower Niger basin. In the dog's homeland it is called *idi n'illeli,* "greyhound of the free nomads."

although varying widely in their coloring, all fit the standard criteria decided on in Verona in 1980 at the general assembly of the International Pure-Bred Dog Federation (FCI, Federation Cynologique Internationale). The fact that these dogs are acknowledged as noble in this village and, indeed, do meet the standard is remarkable: with little concern these beautiful animals walk around the settlement and into the huts. They are cared for and fed in a loving manner. This too differentiates them from Allah's lowest creatures: only dogs who eat garbage are disdained as filthy pigs—the pariahs in villages and cities.

Still, there is a feeling of melancholy at the scene. The "blue knights

Manafi, a noble-
man of the Tuareg,
has traveled five
days on his camel
to find especially
good offspring. He
did not have to
pay for the two
puppies since the
owner considered
it a great honor
that Manafi would
undertake such a
long trip for his
dogs.

The Azawakh

Stature, nature, and beauty have made the Tuareg dog a very desired but nonetheless rare pet in Western industrialized nations. As of January 1, 1981, the azawakh has been recognized as a race by the International Purebred Dog Federation (FCI). The first sentence in the standard description is characteristic of this race: "Especially elegant, the azawakh gives the impression of high nobility."

In the description measurements are given: males may be between sixty-eight and seventy-two centimeters in body height, while females have a maximum body height of sixty-eight centimeters. The narrow head of the dogs should be held up high in a proud manner, then give way to a long muscular neck, which ends in well-placed back shoulders. The eyes are dark brown and almond shaped, their expression is enhanced by the black-pigmented eyelids. The ears, which are thin and have no wrinkles, are at eye level; and form a triangle with a round tip. The azawakhs have an aerodynamic build with an extremely light skeleton. Because their rump is shorter than the rest of their body, their silhouette looks like an elevated rectangle. The hip bones are well defined and the back is straight. The dog appears even more elegant because of its deep chest and extremely high stomach. The tail is very thin and contains no flesh. The front legs, which rest on small paws with strongly curved toes, are steep and straight, almost vertical. The hind legs are wider, and the toes less curved. The skin shows neither dewlap (a fold of skin that hangs from the throat to the chest at the bottom of the neck) nor any other wrinkles, it tightly spans the body so that muscles and vessels are visible.

The hair is straight, short, and fine, without any underwool. It can be any color from light yellow to rust red and is supposed to show white at the tip of the tail, the paws, and the chest. Striped dogs are now accepted as well. Keeping in mind the population's home territory, further liberalization of the FCI standard is in all likelihood merely a matter of time.

Today the azawakhs' survival is threatened because of the political, ecological, and economic conditions in their countries of origin. That is why the Association Burkinabe Idi du Sahel, which is registered in the republic of Burkina Faso, has made it its goal to maintain and further the stock of purebred nomad greyhounds. This internationally assembled association collects money to finance specific projects in the azawakhs' countries of origin. The association learns about conditions and developments in these countries, undertakes expeditions to them, and gives advice on the import of azawakhs. The fact that there is today a small population of imported azawakhs in the United States and Europe that will increase the genetic potential of the current stock is partly an achievement of this association.

of the desert," a romantic name for the Tuareg derived from their indigo blue face masks, have increasingly turned into sedentary farmers and cattle farmers. Their once timeless model of society has burst after its clash with the twentieth century. The consequences of this are not only suffered by the people; their animals too are affected. The hunt, the original purpose for which azawakhs were bred by Tuareg noblemen, has become a rare and illegal pastime. It is remarkable that the iadan have survived this fundamental transition without any marked changes in behavior or in their willingness to participate in Tuareg life. Of course, one thing is left for them: freedom of movement in the vast space of the savanna.

Aside from occasional hunting, azawakhs have been confined to their second traditional purpose: protecting the herds and goods of their master. This links up to old Tuareg traditions, but the importance of it is new. Already as puppies, greyhounds are acquainted with cattle, especially goats. Placed among the calves of the herd they soon start to view the jumping, bleating animals that gamble about as their own—as greyhounds, albeit strange ones. Much of their long history as hunting companions helps them in their role as protector. With the Tuareg they learned to defend the property of their master, whether objects or animals. On the hunt,

In contrast to other dogs greyhounds are considered to be pure by Muslims. Only animals that feed off garbage are seen as filthy. Greyhounds are fed lovingly and are taken seriously as individuals. For Ayad, the moodiness of his dogs is a sign of their nobility.

they themselves never killed but merely encircled the game that men then killed. And the loneliness of the desert facilitates the development of character traits that were desired in the past and still are today: loyalty and protective instincts.

These traits are highly developed among their race. Already as puppies the young azawakhs forms ties to their master and their master's family. Those who threaten them have to expect an attack from the iadan—even children and other dogs and pets. Mistrust of foreigners, originating from their harsh environment, is thus one of the most noticeable character traits of this race. However, mistrust does not necessarily lead to aggression. Those accepted as guests by the azawakh's master will not be threatened. Yet, as a Tuareg proverb warns, if the master is aggressive his dog will not be peaceful. We encountered both throughout our travels.

Remarkable about this is also the constant recognition that the history of humans is so obviously connected to that of their dogs in this region. Where these dogs originally came from remains hidden under the thick veil of past millennia. Dog researchers are engaged in a controversy over whether the ancient ancestors of the azawakhs were Asian herder dogs who bred with African pariahs and southern wolves, or whether the ancestors were Egyptian greyhounds, the so-called tesem dogs, who paired with dogs from little Asia imported by Greeks.

Dog researchers estimate that these dogs have lived with humans for the past four or five thousand years. It is possible that today's iadan separated from their related northern sloughis about two thousand years ago because this was required by their masters' way of life. From this separate path of civilization, which led into the lonely desert, there developed a culture whose last peaks we can still experience in Burkina Faso. How it presented itself one hundred years earlier we can conjecture from the description by the great animal researcher Alfred Brehm. Shortly before the turn of the century he wrote in *Tierleben*:

> Among the tribes of Arabs at the edge of the Sahara there exists a proverb: A good hawk, a fast dog, a noble horse are worth more than twenty women—and one understands the significance of this proverb once one has lived amongst these people. All inhabitants of the desert, the sedentary ones as well as the nomads, honor the greyhound in an unusual fashion. It was not possible for me to acquire a greyhound since the people were absolutely unwilling to commit to such a trade.

While other dogs barely receive enough food and are roughly pushed out of the tents, the greyhound sleeps at the side of his master on rugs and sometimes can even be found in the master's bed. One tries to humor him when he is cross, all because his flaws are considered to be a sign of his nobility. One finds pleasure in adorning him with all sorts of jewelry, places collars and shells on him and decorates him with numerous talisman to protect him from the look of the evil eye.

This is true to this day: when Taikoussou, Ayad's dog, was well along in her pregnancy her owner ordered new bowls for the dogs from the "blacksmith." Blacksmiths among the Tuareg are members of small groups who not only work as metalworkers but also as furriers, cobblers, and carvers. They also make saddles, bags, and pots. Aside from their manual abilities they possess magical powers, enabling them to do favors for their patrons. When Ayad ordered the bowls for his dogs, the smith did not forget to decorate the handles with artful poker work using a hot blade to protect the dogs from the evil eye. However, this is only effective against *dschinns*, the evil spirits; it does not prevent conflicts among the race. We observed with amusement how, shortly before giving birth, Taikoussou drove her brother Boum away from the bowls with mad growls.

Ayad has ordered bowls from the blacksmith for Taikoussou's puppies. When finished the bowls are branded with artful designs that not only are for decoration but also act as magic to protect the dogs from the "evil eye" of jealous neighbors.

When we returned through the land of the azawakhs several weeks later, we saw how these dogs had found their way into so many hearts: effortlessly they glided through the tall, dry grass, jumped over shrubs, dared our car which they by now recognized, to a short race, and then slowly walked back to their village with elevated tails. They are not yet a mirage in the sand of the desert. They still exist—the noble dogs of the blue knights of the Sahara.

BORNEO

Among Hunters in the
Rain Forest

The tropical rain forest, filled with life
from its roots to the crowns of the trees,
is a place of death where the fight for food is the top priority.
BIRUTE M. F. GALDIKAS, *REFLECTIONS OF EDEN*

While Erfin finishes the hardwood spear tip in his dim log hut, the dead body rests at his feet as though asleep. Erfin is working on a small wooden blade. He lovingly sharpens both sides and on the area in between he etches a small figure. Threatening, it displays its chest to the observer.

Erfin is convinced that this guard, the *hampatong,* will protect the dead body against all the unknown powers that will threaten him now more than at any time during his life. This is why he keeps polishing the mystical wood with practiced movements of his hands.

Finally, he carefully ties the carved blade to the long wooden spear using a palm-leaf fiber. He then carries the body and the finished weapon to the village center in front of his hut. Here he meets Leo, the chief of the small Punan settlement here in the northeastern highland of Borneo. The hunter passes the body to Leo and then follows him to the prepared grave, a short distance away from the ten-family settlement, carrying the spear like a scepter.

Together the two men spread banana leaves and bark in the grave and place the body on them. It rests on its left side, where the heart used to

Previous page: The Punan and their dogs, an indispensable partnership

Facing page: The dogs find the game and trap it until the hunter arrives at the scene to kill it with his spear. The hunt for wild boar, animals that are well able to defend themselves, can be dangerous.

Right: Each Punan owns a small pack (between five and nine) of dogs for hunting. At many huts people erect sleeping platforms for the dogs.

With lianas and soft strips of bark, hunters quickly transform an animal who has been killed into an easy-to-carry backpack. After all, a full-grown boar weighs about 150 kilograms.

beat. Erfin carefully places the spear on the dead body and on that a patterned blue cloth to protect the body from the earth, which he and Leo now pile onto it. On the flat grave Leo then places three rocks the size of a fist, arranged like a pyramid. They signal that this is the place where someone rests who has passed from their community into the realm of ancestors, shadows, and spirits. Good-bye Bentschong. He had just turned nine and he was Erfin's favorite hunting companion: a dog.

Researchers call the religion of the Punan animistic; it differentiates them from the Muslim or Christian tribes in Borneo. Originally a nomad hunter-gatherer tribe, the Punans live primarily in the north and in the hilly center of Borneo and probably descend from the Mali. These fragile, tender people do not look at their existence as separate from death, whose shadow is always with them. They do not distinguish between the natural and the spiritual. This is why they also do not have concrete beliefs regarding life after death. For the Punan there is only the light and the dark side of reality. People can travel back and forth between these two. They do this exactly like the animals that are closest to them. For the Punan these animals are their dogs, their indispensable hunting companions. Bentschong, for example, killed over one hundred pigs for Erfin. The symbolic spear and the cloth of his master were placed in his grave as a token of appreciation for this.

In the Punan religion, a daily part of Punan life, nothing happens by coincidence. There is no sharp dividing line between this life and the next. Like human beings, every animal and every object has a soul, and all souls as spirits influence existence in the present and the future. This be-

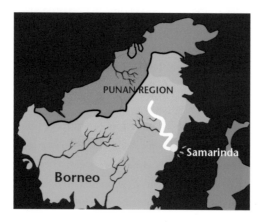

Borneo

With an area of about 750,000 square kilometers, Borneo ranks ahead of Sumatra, Celebes, and Java as the largest of the several thousand islands that are a part of the Republic of Indonesia. After Greenland and New Guinea, it is the third-largest island in the world. Geologically, Borneo belongs to the Malay Archipelago, the chain of islands that stretches along the equator between Australia and Asia.

Two Malaysian states, in the northeastern parts of the island, Sarawak and Sabah, are not under Indonesian rule. Nor is Brunei, whose sultan has become one of the wealthiest men on Earth through the sale of locally extracted oil. These three states occupy about one-third of the island; the remaining territory is divided into the four Indonesian provinces of West, South, East, and Central Kalimantan (the Indonesian name for Borneo). The heart of the island is hilly and covered by rain forests. Steep cliffs and fast-flowing rivers and rapids make the land hard to access—for the original European conquerors, English and Dutch, and for those who today exploit the island's natural resources. The inaccessibility of mountains and cliffs, constantly separating valleys, and foaming waters have to a degree protected the nature of the island from complete destruction.

By now, however, the economies of Sarawak and Sabah are dependent on the export of wood, and in the Indonesian Kalimantan deforestation on an industrial scale continues to expand. Only tiny Brunei protects its rain forests. In the rest of Borneo however, cargo helicopters drop loggers and their various machinery into increasingly isolated areas of the forests. Logging roads are cleared to the next river and huge trees are then transported to collecting sites or straight to the coast. This process destroys not only the habitat of the many animals at home in Borneo, but also the astonishing variety of species found in the rain forests—about 450 different types of trees per hectare—as well as the cultures of original tribes and peoples.

The Punan

Many different peoples live in Borneo. Most are known as Dayaks, a term that does not actually refer to a certain culture or racial group but rather is like the term Indian when applied to the American aboriginal population. In general this term is used to refer to all tribes in the heartland of Borneo that are not Islamic. Therefore Dayaks occasionally are thought to include the Punan, who are then referred to as mountain Dayaks. In the original sense, however, there is a difference between the Punan, who are solely hunter-gatherers and the Dayak tribes, who also engage in agriculture.

The people of Punan, who live primarily in Sarawak and North Borneo, were described by the early discoverers of the island as purely nomadic. Today this only applies to some Punan tribes and clans in inaccessible areas, especially those far from the coast. In the present day, most of the Punan live in sedentary huts and log cabins that are modeled after Dayak houses, even if their construction is not as artistic. Although the origin of this people is unknown, anthropologists consider them to be a hunting community that early on split from the Malay—one of the three large population groups of Borneo—and who then pursued a socioculturally different way of life, undisturbed in the dense rain forest in Borneo's heartland.

The Punan's traditional way of life is now in danger: the forests continue to be cut down and the land tamed for modern civilization. For the Punan this means more frequent and more intense contact with civilization. The loss of identity among tribes can be seen from the fact that in certain areas of Borneo the term Punan has started to be applied to all humans who enter the jungle, whether for short or longer expeditions.

lief and many of its accompanying rituals can be found not only in Borneo but also in Siberia and South America among Eskimos and bushmen. Scholars believe that in the Stone Age similar beliefs developed in many places on Earth.

In fact the Punan dogs might have originated in the Stone Age. They show us how constructed the concept of race is, a concept that breeders in the West use so convincingly. To the Punan these animals, which European cynologists have often simply referred to as pariahs, as mixtures, are their own race.

Be it the dead Bentschong, be it Lojan, his team companion, be it Urong, Lipan, Mi-Ap, or Poa—all of them and their sixty relatives in this Punan settlement are about fifty centimeters tall and have a blunt head with a flat, cone-shaped skull. And, as if constantly contemplating life, the entire race exhibits wrinkles on their foreheads. We saw these dogs in other settlements as well as in the Punan village.

Most of the time their short, silky hair has either a light or dark chestnut red coloring, although some animals are all black, and others are black with white spots, sand colored, or beige and white. All have fine and attentive sharp ears, and their dark, almond-shaped and slightly slanted eyes constantly observe their surroundings.

These dogs have another characteristic in common: they never really bark. They cry and whimper, they hiss and purr, sing and yodel, pant and scream. But they don't bark. Their owners have adjusted their interactions with their dogs to the dog's articulation. Already the puppies are enticed with soft, melodic noises: "Woe-woe-woe-woeah" or "Wu-wu-wuah!" Grown dogs are called with

a long "Aiiiah," a sound that carries far even in the dense jungle.

There is no doubt for the observer that these dogs, living in many villages of the Punan and also kept with the nomad part of this people, are a race—even according to the scientific definition of this term. Zoologists like the German pet researcher Wolf Herre and his colleague, Klaus Löhle, a researcher for the Humboldt Institute, have clearly defined the term *race* over the past decades. According to them a race is consitituted by a type of animal with certain characteristics such as similarities in build, character, and behavior; clear differences between them and other races of the same animal group; and the ability to be bred with others of its race and pass these characteristics on to future generations. All this is true for to the dogs of the Punan.

But by no means are they to be found solely in Borneo, and we are probably not the first to have found these dogs interesting. In the nineteenth century the world traveler and dog lover Max Siber found their trail. In 1892 he reported on them in the "Central Paper for Hunting and Dog Fans" (Centralblatt für Jagd- und Hundeliebhaber): "The dog has upright standing ears, a curled tail and an elevated stomach. Its basic color

Punan dogs are the best playmates for children.

In the jungle of Borneo, the dogs of the Punan look so alike that one could consider them their own race. They're reminiscent of Australian dingoes or African basenjis. Especially lovable are the "worried" wrinkles they always have on their foreheads.

Opposite: Small, stocky, and constantly alert, it seems these dogs were made for the hunt in the dense forest. At the age of six months the Punan dog is taken on its first hunting expedition. In the pack it learns from the more experienced dogs.

is a yellow-red, often with white spots, sometimes entirely white and in rare cases entirely black or blue." Siber also reported that the natives "use this dog for hunting," and observed that "this dog cries more often than it barks." However, he did not discover this dog in Borneo, but rather found it in Africa: "This dog is at home with all the tribes in Africa. The most common form is the animal that is known from ancient Egypt as 'King Sufi's race.'"

It is true that pictures of these dogs appeared in hieroglyphs from Egypt that date back to 6,000 B.C., and deep in southern Africa at the Sambesi a fragment of a relief was found that shows these dogs on a hunt for apes and zebras. So are these far-traveled citizens of the world, or are they dogs who in the early times of all cultures developed in the same or a very similar fashion in various tribes?

This is another reason why this encounter was so fascinating for us: dogs from Africa, as old as the Great Pyramid of Khufu (where pictures of these dogs can also be found), crossed this way at the close of the second millennium in the dense jungle of Borneo. Who are they? For only about a half century have they had a name in at least one part of the world: basenji, which in the language of the pygmies in the Congo area roughly means "the little bush animal." And cynologists have only recently developed a theory that explains how such similar dogs came to develop on two separate continents.

In this respect dog fans probably have much to thank Eberhard Trumler for. He was a dog researcher, friend, breeder, and expert who passed away in 1991 and had for a long time been held in little regard by academics as an amateur in the field. He pointed out the connection among different types of wolves all over the world who had to adapt their instinctive behavior to varying conditions, therein giving rise to the first race of dogs. The pariah dogs in the north and south of Eurasia and Africa are among these. In time-intensive cross-breeding attempts of jackals, wolves, and dingoes, Trumler used behavior and build of the animals on his large estate to prove their "first-born right," and to prove that they were the ancestors of the nearly five hundred different races that exist today. He continued to explain this in books, lectures, and essays throughout his life.

Trumler was the first to connect hundreds of single observations to a larger and plausible picture, which by now has gained scientific recognition. In this the dogs of the Punan, our Borneo basenjis, have their own place as well. This is because such animals are found not only at the southern shore of the South China Sea, but also on two other big islands fifteen hundred kilometers farther east in New Guinea. There, in 1956,

they were first described as New Guinea dingoes and received their own scientific name: *Canis hallstromi*, the dog from the Hallstrom era. The British had already named the animal New Guinea Singing Dogs, a name known to European sailors since 1606. Today these dogs are no longer considered a separate race, but are classified as a special type of dingo that, as Bernhard Grzimek pointed out in the 1970s, has "family ties to the Indonesian house dogs." Because of this, today the singing dog from New Guinea has also scientifically found its way back into the lap of the dog family—*Canis lupus*—just like the wolf and all dogs, with an addition: *familiaris hallstromi*—a "family wolf" from the Stone Age. The New Guinea dog resembles its cousin from Borneo, as do many basenji types in central Africa; its description by Eberhard Trumler thus fits all three: "a small, relatively short-legged dog that in some aspects resembles a Pomeranian; this is accentuated through its tail that is curled above its back. It has short, upright-standing ears, and a relatively short, blunt snout. Its coloring

Although the dogs receive the best meat of the bounty as their share, and even when, with the help of their dogs, the hunters kill animals every day, the dogs receive meat only every three days. The Punan believe that otherwise their dogs would become too slow.

is similar to a dingo's. The white paws, the white tip of the tail, as well as a patch on the breast and an occasionally white back of the nose indicate an early stage of domestication, much as with the dingo."

Our expedition to the Punan seemed to become a voyage to the Stone Age in that this primarily nomadic people still exist in the harsh conditions of the rain forest in the way our European ancestors did millennia ago: as hunters and gatherers who do not cultivate the soil. Hunting with dogs is considered to be the most effective way of obtaining food. Before the dogs were included, the Punan hunted with only a blowpipe. Yet this method only works when hunting small animals like birds, snakes, and small monkeys. The effects of the poison starts too late with bigger game such as boar, resulting in the animal's escape or attack. This is why dogs have such an important position in the Punan's societal hierarchy.

It is the dog's responsibility to find, pursue, and trap the game until the hunter is able to kill it with his spear. We experienced how successful this method is on a boar hunt to which our friends invited us. Boar are well able to defend themselves and find perfect living conditions in the rain forests and mangrove thickets of Borneo. They are killed only by the natives of the inland because the mostly Islamic population living at the coast does not consider the meat of these animals to be pure.

The great number of boar almost provoked a war in 1954 between the coastal population and the inland tribes. In that year the boar migrated in such masses from the north of the island to the south that the Punan and other mountain tribes massacred the animals to prevent them from eating all the tribes' food of roots, fruits, and wild vegetables. Because of this, in conjunction with the Punan's refusal to use the boar as food, the rivers were blocked farther down by the many cadavers, and the Muslims, in response, sent troops against those responsible for this unusual flooding, which for them represented an ecological catastrophe. Contaminated by the poison of the impure animal cadavers, the water of the rivers was no longer pure.

Today boar are not found in Borneo in such large numbers. This is not so much because the Punan and other tribes hunted them to extinction, as because of the brutal deforestation of a tropical rain forest that was once the second-largest cohesive area of forest in the world. The republic of Indonesia makes money at the expense of the environment and the traditional way of life of the many people and tribes that live within its borders in Borneo, just as in West Irian, the western half of New Guinea. And Malaysia, to which the northwest of Borneo belongs, practices even more deforestation than Indonesia.

But for now boar can still be found, as can pythons and other snakes, fowl, moose, and smaller types of monkeys; these animals are the game for all the mountain tribes. Other animals are endangered and threatened by extinction in Borneo; the orangutan, one of the three big apes (its natural habitat is only here and in the neighboring Sumatra); the rhinoceros; and the wild sunda cattle. All of them are losing their habitat to deforestation—and one day the Punan probably will too.

In the way it is practiced by Leo and his tribal brothers, the hunt does not matter in the Russian roulette of the rain forest. On each hunt the Punan kill only as many animals as they need for themselves, their village, and their dogs. The dogs receive their share of the kill, and by no means do they get only the worst pieces. However, meat is given to the dogs only every three days, otherwise—so the hunters say—the animals would be too lazy for the hunt. The dogs seem to accept their mainly vegetarian diet without too much resistance.

Whatever food they get, the dogs deserve. On the hunt they do remarkable amounts of work. First, they have to find the trail, after which Leo and the other hunters are in constant vocal contact with the dogs. By the dogs' different sounds the hunters can recognize what type of game the pack is following at the time. Once the dogs are on a trail, the hunters encourage them through calls that are barely distinguishable from the hunting sounds of the running dogs. "The dogs do not understand our language, so we have to speak to them in theirs," Leo explains.

When the pack has finally trapped the game, the hunting sounds of the dogs change into a triumphant song. Immediately the hunters come in; quickly and almost noiselessly they run through the dense rain forest. Once they reach the trapped animal, one well-placed jab with the spear is usually all it takes. But the hunt is dangerous for both man and dog since wild boar are well equipped to defend themselves. Many dogs have scars left by the tusks of the boar. The Punan attend to these wounds with steamed healing herbs they collect in the giant natural pharmacy of the rain forest.

Dogs training for the hunt start at an early age. Only a complete understanding between man and dog secures success. This is why in every pack of dogs, there is always one experienced leader, several dogs with some hunting experience, and about two or three newcomers who in learning by doing are instructed for their future job.

Each Punan household has five or six dogs, yet these are not all hunting dogs. They also live like members of the family as pets, with rights equal to those of their human counterparts. Some families even erect separate sleeping platforms for the dogs inside or around the hut. They are excellent playmates for children, and many women carry their favorite animal around under their arms. This treatment of dogs is an unbelievable extravagance for a people who continually have to fight for their daily survival against the powerful and threatening forces of nature. Only the high esteem given to the dogs as helpers in this fight can explain their position of privilege. How far the respect for the *asu* (the Punan's term for "dog") goes can be seen by the important role the dogs play in traditional rituals, and the fact that the most common tattoo among the Punan depicts a highly stylized dog.

Naturally, the best hunting dogs are taken especially good care of. They are also used for planned breeding, which is only done for performance

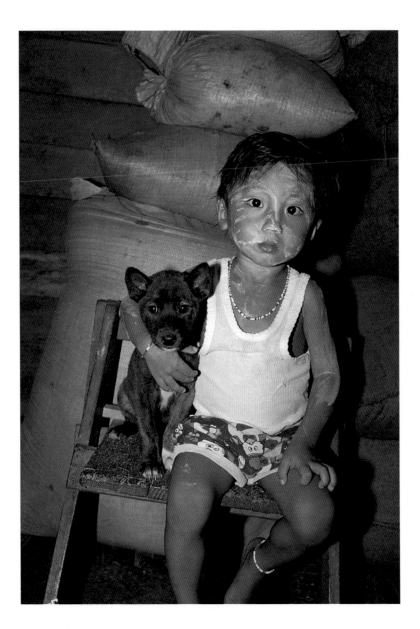

Dogs are considered members of the family and are allowed in the huts at all times. Little Nissa has already chosen his future hunting companion.

characteristics and not for the dog's appearance. The color of the fur, for example, does not matter to the Punan, color being at most a question of personal preference. All dogs have names, special names that are different from those used for humans. Only female dogs are collared and leashed, and this is done so that they can be kept under control when in heat so that undesirable reproduction can be avoided.

Males are free to move about since they obey every command. When a single hunter wants to go into the forest for hunting with his spear, he calls the animals by their names to avoid all dogs coming along. Those who are not called accept this, but not happily, desperately whining and always tagging along for a short distance. They are remarkable animals, perfectly adjusted to the people they live with and their way of life—important partners in the fight for survival in the rain forest. There is only one function they do not serve: that of guard dog. This is because they are so used to humans that they never question them, not even strangers.

It is not clear from where the Punan first got their dogs. Nor is it known how long they have been living with the hunting dogs in this mutually beneficial relationship. Researchers hypothesize that the hunting people of Borneo have only used dogs for a few centuries, maybe even for as short a time as a few generations. In the "predog era" of Borneo (an actual term) the blowpipe alone, filled with a deadly mixture of paralyzing poisons from the upas tree (Antiaris toxicaria), was used for the hunt. The blowpipe is still used, but only hunting with the dogs guarantees that the entire village will be fed.

One theory claims that the Punan acquired their dogs through contact with other tribes and peoples in the coastal regions, or that, through barter with rice farmers or merchants, the dogs came from one of the many islands surrounding Borneo. This theory is countered by the racial perfection of the Punan dogs in build, character, and ability, traits that are unattainable in that short a time, as well as the belief of some sociologists who hypothesize that these nomad hunters were once a sedentary people. Why would the Punan, having abandoned dog breeding when they became a sedentary tribe, resort to it again later?

If it were possible to discover the history of these dogs, it would also be possible to draw further conclusions about the history of humankind, because for at least fourteen thousand years the evolution of Homo sapiens has been closely linked to that of Canis lupus, a symbiotic relationship that offers advantages to both sides. There is no other comparable example in the history of nature or culture of this symbiotic relationship. The evolution of humans has always encouraged that of the dog and vice versa. This relationship is especially evident in Borneo, where we seemed to have stepped back into the Stone Age.

The Punan's expertise in dog caretaking and breeding, within their own culture and worldwide, is shown not only in the quality and performance of their dogs, but also in the fact that the Punan dogs have been highly desired animals all over Borneo for quite some time. Members of other peoples and tribes continue to come here to trade with the Punan in order to acquire good hunting dogs.

The dogs of the Punan Busang, one particular tribe of this people, are

Often the Punan sit together to chew betel nuts. On these occasions they often give the dogs tender massages. After all, the animals need to remain agile for the hunt.

especially in demand. In 1965 a sociologist reported that a Kayan chief traded iron, salt, and tobacco with the master of a particularly good Busang dog. This chief wanted the dog so badly that he even rented a helicopter to complete the trade as quickly as possible. Today, continuously pushed by civilization, the Punan also take money for their dogs. After all, with money they can buy goods from loggers and Dayak villages at the lower banks of the rivers—goods like dried coconut flakes and textiles (until recently the Punan still used softened bark for their loincloths).

The Dayaks, who live closer to the coast, also keep dogs. Bigger animals with a wider skull, these dogs do not have the high hunting and breeding quality of the Punan dogs. At times they seem to be pure dingoes from faraway Australia: the same red, short fur, mistrustful character, intelligence, long rump and a deep and broad chest, and a slightly big head with the wide ears. Is this where the settlers who brought dogs to the fifth continent three thousand, or perhaps even thirteen thousand years ago came from, where they then digressed again? This too is one of the questions that neither cynologists nor sociologists have been able to answer thus far.

We did not find the answer either. However, we did develop the conviction that we had met people and animals who are still very close to the origins of their respective species. The breeding of the dogs was a small step for the Punan, but a big one for humankind: when the first hunters from the Stone Age found their canine companions they made the hunt much more effective.

According to an ancient legend, the Punan created their dogs themselves—from the resin of a eucalyptus tree. The creature was supposed to have quick legs and a good nose, and it needed to be able to speak so it could call to the hunter. In response to their requests, a god breathed into the figure and, thereby, gave the dog life.

In the legends of the Punan, we do find an answer to the question of where their hunting companions came from. Leo told us the following story:

A long time ago two hunters of the Punan tribe were traveling through the jungle of Borneo. They were out for hours, yet, as happened much of the time, they were having no luck with the hunt. Whenever they did find game, it managed to get away in the dense forest. Exhausted, they rested under a eucalyptus tree and contemplated which animal would be useful for them during the hunt. It should have a good nose to pick up a trail quickly. It needed to be fast, in order to be able to trap the game. It should have sharp teeth in order to be able to grab the bounty. And it would need to be able to talk so it could call the hunters to the right place. They collected the resin of the eucalyptus tree and then shaped such a creature: the dog. Upon their requests a god breathed life into their creature and this is how it came about that the Punan from then on were able to hunt so successfully—with the dog at their side.

The Basenji

The small hunting dog who is thought to belong to the schensi dogs of Africa and Asia has been bred in Europe since 1936. The first basenjis to be imported from Congo to England were named Bongo and Bokoto. When they were displayed for the first time in 1937 at the Crufts Dog Show in London special security forces had to be employed to keep the visitors moving past the basenji cages: that's how big a stir these nonbarking dogs caused.

The basenji, who has been recognized as a race in the United States since 1943 and shortly thereafter by the International Purebred Dog Federation (FCI), as a purebred animal, has only African (no Asian) ancestors. This is probably because relatives of the basenjis—in Borneo, for example—were discovered much later than the branch found in central Africa, and from which the name was derived. Through the breeding process's strict standards, the purebred basenji is now very different from its namesakes in their home countries.

However, the lovable and loyal basenjis have retained many characteristics of the original schensi dogs: attention to surroundings, being in heat only once a year (a characteristic of many "primitive" dogs), and the wrinkles in the forehead that make their faces appear forever worried. Because they have passed on their appearance and character to other generations, they fulfill the main requirement for being recognized as a race, even though their breeding basis in Europe is extremely small: it basically traces back to only about eleven dogs, who were imported to Europe in 1936 and successive years. For now, the number of people who love this dog is still small. The most famous basenji owner is probably Juliana, former queen of the Netherlands.

PATAGONIA

The Right Hand of the Gauchos

Aside from the higher intelligence and learning capacity
it is especially the lower nervousness and better stress capacity of
the mixed dog that enables a higher level of training.
KONRAD LORENZ, MAN MEETS DOG, 1965

From the high, rough wall of the Perito Moreno glacier, a block of ice weighing several tons tumbles into Lake Argentino. Soon after, Alef barks and jumps into the ice-cold mountain water thrilled to be paddling among the ice. Alef belongs to Claudio, the manager of the Glacier Hotel. He was originally a city dog from tropical Buenos Aires and only came to western Patagonia a few years ago with his master. Because of this one might regard this not entirely purebred descendant of European spaniels as a typical Argentinean. Much like him, all of his canine relatives in Patagonia have found a new home in the largely uninhabited southern tip of the American subcontinent far from their original countries. Unlike Alef, however, most of these relatives are working dogs.

This is because Patagonia is sheep country where about one-third of Argentina's sixty million sheep graze. Some of the nearly fifty million cattle of the country also graze on the more fertile pastures. To herd, protect, and keep these other animals moving, dogs were and are necessary. The first settlers of the 1880s and 1890s brought these working dogs with them from their native countries.

They came from Wales, Scotland, and England. They crossed the Andes and came through Chile; they arrived by ship from Naples, or sometimes from the German Bremerhaven, to a wild, new, and unknown coast. Land-less peasants from Spain, as well as escaped Russian serfs, belonged to this incoming army of immigrants. And some of them came with their dogs, dogs from whom descended a variety of dogs who over time have developed equal abilities—the shepherd dogs of Patagonia.

It is thus no miracle that on the fourteen-thousand-kilometer-long journey through the vast country we met many old acquaintances from Europe in their new jobs. The different settlements in the region are too far apart from one another, the *estancias*, or farms of the herd owners, are too isolated for a physically distinct dog population to have evolved in a few dozen decades.

Not-quite-purebred Newfoundlands cross our path, as well as Labradors, foxhounds, and mastiffs. Sometimes a dog appears to have come di-

Previous page: A spectacular exhibition of the forces of nature at the southernmost end of the world. The Perito Moreno glacier moves into Lake Argentino at a rate of about one meter per day. Thunder sounds as the wall of ice crashes into the lake, one piece at a time.

rectly from the Lüneburg Heath—a Pastor Aleman, a German shepherd. We see mountain dogs from the Pyrenees and the Abruzzi, but most often dogs from the border region, dogs from that area that lies between England and Scotland and is regarded as the home of most terriers and many shepherds: Border collies especially. With many of the dogs, however, ancestery is hard to discern.

All dogs here serve as noble working dogs. Next to horses they are the most important companions of their masters; they are the right hand of the gauchos and the *estancieros* (sheep farmers). We did not see descendants of the original dogs of the Indians, and can conclude that they must have died along with the humans who were once the masters of this country. Most of the native Indian inhabitants fell victim to a bloody war that the army of the Europeanizing Argentinean government waged against them between 1877 and 1879. Today there are very few pure-blooded heirs of these ancient peoples, only mestizos, people of mixed European and Indian ancestry who settled in this country in several waves after the "cleansing" of the area. With the destruction of the hunting nomads who lived in the grass and scrub desert of Patagonia, nomad languages and cultures were lost as well. And of the animals of the Mapuche or the Tehuelche all that remain are the descriptions of early travelers, zoologists, and sociologists.

"Extremely wild looking" was the description the American G. M. Allen gave in 1920 of what he called the Patagonian dog, the Indians' hunting dog that could still occasionally be found in Allen's day. Medium tall, with rough, scraggly hair, these dogs resembled "a small wolf. Behind their shoulders their fur was soft and short, in front however it was thick and extended like the mane of a lion." Only rarely do we see mixed dogs that possibly still carry the gene of this dog.

The dog's southern cousin, the Fuegian dog, is extinct too. The Fuegian dog was the "fire-country dog," a companion in the hunt and on fishing expeditions. According to a description dating back to 1840, above the

Most of the dogs in Patagonia are the descendants of different herder-dog races that immigrants brought with them over two hundred years ago: collies from Scotland, mountain dogs from the Pyrenees, mastiffs from Italy, bobtails from England, and shepherds from Germany.

dark fur over each eye this dog had "a white spot with reddish-yellow hair." European interest in this dog was as low as that in the Patagonian dog, because unlike the Europeans' own dogs, the dogs of the Indians were silent hunters: they went after game without barking. For this reason the white immigrants preferred the dogs they had brought with them.

The early gauchos were used to loud hunting and guard dogs. It was these freedom-loving nomads who in the nineteenth century carried the burden of battling the Spanish acquisition of South America, a burden that was not considered dishonorable. The few surviving Indians assimilated until they eventually disappeared in the flood of white conquerors. Only about five percent of today's population of Argentina—the mestizos to be precise—still have at least some Indian blood. On one of our expeditions we became acquainted with a family with this heritage.

This family lives on a picturesque self-sufficient farm with some vegetable cultivation, horses, and some cattle. Because of the links to their Indian Mapuche tradition, they sometimes still go hunting. Not all mestizos admit their Indian heritage, but our hosts do. Despite this heritage, in the course of their family history they acquired the very unusual last name Beissman, which indicates some German heritage.

But they too are no longer assisted by Patagonian dogs on their hunt for the South American ostriches, the *nandos*. Instead they hunt with *galgos*, descendants of Spanish greyhounds. Special hunting packs of dogs are rare in Patagonia, even for the rich, largely because in the low-growing vegeta-

The Border collie is among the most famous dog races in the world. According to the latest studies, it is even the most intelligent race of dog in the world.

tion of the boundless flat expanses, there is hardly any game left to be found.

With a hunt for predators, however, the gauchos have the guard dogs of their herds trap these archrivals of the cattle farmers until they can be killed with one precise shot. As a warning to those left alive, cadavers of these animals are mounted on poles at the side of the roads that lead through grazing areas. The life here is tough and the people cannot afford a loss in cattle. For generations they have lived under these conditions with their dogs at their side.

One or two hectares of this sparse earth here in southern Patagonia feed only one sheep, mostly a sheep adapted to this harsh environment, mixed from different breeds—Corriedales, Lincolns, and Romney and Marshsheep. While pure wool sheep like merinos may deliver better wool, they require a standard of soil that is not available, not to mention their inability to survive in the harsh climate. So only sheep with a rougher and thicker fleece than the purebred sheep are options for the shepherds. While such sheep provide good meat, their wool has proven hard to sell on world markets over the past few years.

Still, sheep shearing remains the highlight of the economic year on an estancia. For this event all animals are brought in from the pastures, a job that could not be done without the help of dogs. The shearers who move

Life in Patagonia is hard and the people cannot afford to lose cattle. The remains of killed predators therefore function as macabre memorials—a dramatic warning to the survivors of its kind.

Patagonia is sheep country. In the never-ending expanses of the steppe, dogs guard and direct the herds. As the gauchos say: "My dogs are my companions, just like my horse and the wind. My dogs—they are my right hand!"

from season to season between the estancias, do not own dogs. It is the responsibility of the gauchos and their four-legged companions to gather the sheep in a herd.

Most of the time the male dogs do the shepherding. The gauchos know that females are often just as capable of the task, but most gauchos are nomad travelers, moving from one estancia to another with a pack of up to seven dogs, and a dog with a litter of puppies would pose problems. Thus female dogs are kept almost exclusively by the estancieros or the few gauchos who work permanently on an estancia. The men know what they have in their dogs. This is expressed by Rodrigo, a foreman on Los Corrales, a 10,000 hectare farm with almost 5,000 sheep and 350 cattle: "How would we work without our dogs? They belong to our lives; they are our companions like the horses and the wind."

The wind comes mostly from the west across the Andes mountains; the few trees and bushes bend over and seem to be crawling on the ground. This tough country has fused man and animal closely together. When they work, few words are necessary. The gauchos can rely on the instincts of their dogs: a few whistles and a few spare gestures suffice for communication.

There seems to be an invisible bond between dogs and sheep: two dogs are all that's needed to get a herd to move quickly in the desired direction. To do this the dogs run from the back to the front, constantly changing sides as they pass the sheep. When a flock huddles in front of them because it is supposed to go into the pen, the dogs change their behavior. Their heads lower and the animals seem to almost crawl, although their speed hardly changes even in this slow walk. The sheep move on obediently, all heads turned away from the dog who pushes them forward.

This only takes a few seconds and the gaucho does not have to utter a single command. The sheep show no unrest and the dog shows no exertion. It simply moves back to its spot at the back of the herd where it can observe everything. The nose points sharply downward, set between upward-pointing shoulder blades, and the eyes concentrate on what is ahead—enough intimidation to push those it protects in the desired direction.

As we watched this process, the fascination that comes from the seeming ease of this achievement quickly took hold of us: instinct and intelligence of human and dog are combined here in a wonderful manner for the mastering of a common task. The dogs do most of the work; the humans simply transmit their wishes, which it is up to to the animals to fulfill. However, there are certain taboos: pinching and other minor physical attacks are allowed; biting, grabbing, and frantic chasing are prohibited. The dogs are thus allowed only threatening gestures that suffice to steer the sheep who do not voluntarily cooperate.

It is as if the dogs' talent for their work is in their mothers' milk. They do not receive special training; rather they learn from the older animals and develop their skills on the job. Among the dogs that we met on the many estancias, this held true for all of them, no matter the breed. Race, at least in the meaning of physical appearance, matters little to the Gauchos anyway. The animals need a certain physical size to command respect from the herd, but other than that only their effectiveness is important.

Whether a dog is purebred matters little to the gauchos. The four-legged "immigrants" of earlier days interbred and eventually became the most vital helpers of these legendary riding herders.

Patagonia

Patagonia is the southernmost stretch of land on the South American continent, starting at about the 39° south latitude. The border between the smaller Chilean part and the much larger Argentinean part runs along the highly glaciated cordillera of the southern Andes mountain range that divides Patagonia like a backbone into north and south, two different climate zones. The Chilean west Patagonia is humid and chilly, part of which is densely covered by forested mountains with deep fjords and numerous islands along the coast. Argentinean east Patagonia, covering about eight hundred thousand square kilometers, is a sloped land that decreases in height in steppes as it comes closer to the Atlantic—this was the main area of our expedition. Close to the Andes there are still numerous lakes and rivers that have cut deeply into the valleys. In the highlands there is mostly desert and steppe.

For scientists this country is one of about two hundred biogeographical provinces of Earth, common habitats for typical animal and plant groups. Here in Patagonia everything has adapted to the dry climate. The country was discovered in 1520 by the Portuguese seafarer Ferdinand Magellan, who called the area the country of the *patagones,* the "big footed." Perhaps he had discovered the footprints of the Indians, who wrapped their feet in guanaco fur. Around 1780, a settlement was slowly started by emigrating Europeans and descendants of Spanish conquistadors from the northern part of South America.

Because the poor soil and stormy winds don't allow for the cultivation of plants, in this area—which constitutes one-third of the territory of Argentina but is only home to about 3 percent of its population—cattle farming is the primary source of livelihood.

The cattle farming, which has become more intensive in the past one hundred years, has, in spite of Patagonia's size, led to changes in the vegetation and fauna of this country: the domesticated animals need ever larger quantities of water and food and thereby force the nondomesticated planteaters into hopeless competition. As the competition leads to a population decrease, predators are forced to look for their prey among the animals of the herds, and thereby initiate their decimation at the hands of humans.

The original inhabitants of this land, Patagonian tribes of Indians like the Tehuelche, were killed in the last century by whites, especially in the tribal wars that started in 1879 under General Julio A. Roca, who went down in history as "the last of the conquistadors."

Science terms such a biological process the "heterosis effect." Without special manipulations of breeding by humans, mixed dogs are likely to be more robust, more able to learn, more adaptable, and less problematic than purebred dogs. Interbreeding also increases dogs' resistance to illnesses and their fertility rate.

Here in rough Patagonia the average estanciero has to be not only a hard worker, but also good at math. For example, Frederico, the owner of Los Corrales, along with his wife, the supervisor Rodrigo, and five part-time employed gauchos, annually earns a little under ten thousand dollars—if all goes well. But, things can go wrong very quickly. The previous winter almost one-quarter of the country's sheep died, either freezing to death or suffocating under snow in narrow valleys that seemed to offer refuge. The estancieros were not all hard hit: although some lost all their animals, others lost only five percent of their herds. Frederico was among the lucky ones.

The fact that he was still able to bring many of his small herds to safety was largely due to his dogs. They were not able to save all the animals scattered throughout the large area, but they did their best. It took them two hours to bring an endangered flock of about five hundred sheep to the safety of the pen. For men on horseback using no dogs this would have taken at least half a day—time that the harsh winter did not allow. It's no wonder that Frederico cares for his dogs as though they were members of his family.

The gauchos do not train their dogs, but rather rely entirely on their inherent guarding instincts. The dogs go about their work with great enthusiasm.

Because of the poor soil only few cattle are kept in Patagonia. The cattle who do live here spend their entire lives out in the wild. Working with these cattle is a special challenge for the dogs.

Not all the small estancieros of Patagonia are as content as Frederico is. The tough competition and often dismal demand for their products forces them to maximize efficiency and ration their own provisions where possible, a process that counts dogs among its victims. On some estancias it is only the gauchos who still own dogs and who stubbornly refuse to try the "new and even better" purebred shepherd dogs of which they might have heard.

We too at first found out about this supposedly new dog only in the form of a rumor. This is typical for Patagonia, the Argentinean part of which is three times the area of Germany. Only about one million people live here. Some of these we met, but many others heard about us and the purpose of our expedition via radio, the most important form of communication for the estancieros.

The shortwave message we received one day said that we should pay attention to the new race of dog. The animals came from Australia and were probably crossbred with dingoes, the greyhounds of the fifth continent. They were still unknown in the north but we would be able to find them in the south. A little later the desert radio transmitted an address: the estancia Monte Dinero, located at the Cabo Virgines, truly the southernmost point of continental Argentina, on the same latitude as the Falkland Islands.

On Christmas Day we arrived there and, feeling like intruders, we knocked on the door of the Fenton family. In spite of Christmas celebration and siesta time we were immediately asked to come in and once again

The Gauchos

The gauchos, the legendary freedom-hungry, lonely men in the vast steppe, are a living myth deeply rooted in the Argentinean self-image. They originally were loners who in the early period of Spanish colonization in the seventeenth century crossed the borders of civilization and chose a life in the freedom of the untouched south. They initially lived in peace with the Indian population. *Gaucho* is actually an Indian word and means "orphan." To this day there are significantly more mestizos living among the gauchos than among any other population group.

A fundamental change in the gaucho lifestyle was precipitated by the division of their once boundless home into individual estancias. The free vagabonds turned into unwanted bums. Many of them joined the army where they took part in the destruction of Indians. Others started to work as herders and keepers of the cattle herds on the estancias—becoming a South American counterpart to the cowboy of the north. True machos, gauchos dislike binding relationships and only with rare exceptions have regular family ties.

Charles Darwin met them on his voyage around the world in 1833 and described what still holds true: "The gauchos are known for being excellent riders. The thought to get thrown off a horse—regardless of what the horse is doing—never crosses their mind. Among them the trademark of a good rider is when a man can handle an untamed horse and when, if the horse falls, the rider lands on his two feet."

Only rarely are these riding herders employed on a long-term basis on the estancias. More commonly they earn their wages, like the shearer, as traveling seasonal workers. This has shaped their way of life: they are used to covering great distances with little baggage—on their horse, possibly accompanied by a packhorse and their dogs. Essentials include a shotgun, knife, the *boleadora* (an Indian lasso) and their cooking utensils, especially utensils for maté tea, which is prepared with the roasted leaves of the yerba tree. Drinking this stimulating maté is almost ritualistic and is included in nearly every conversation with a gaucho. An orange-sized dried pumpkin holds the maté, which is drunk through a small straw that has a spoonlike sieve at the bottom. Darwin reported this too and listed the four necessities in the life of a gaucho in the field: "food for the horses and dogs, water for everyone, the maté, and meat and wood for a fire." These are still all the gaucho needs in his life on the steppe.

experienced the "corazon patagonico," overflowing hospitality and warmth of the Patagonian heart. Yes, these mysterious new dogs were here. Before we could ask about them they were presented to us: kelpies from Australia, bred by Caroline, the daughter. She immediately impressed us with a display in a nearby meadow, of the abilities of this shepherd race, but we were even more impressed in the house when she presented the youngest generation of her breeding attempts. The puppies were just four weeks old. Black and tan or red and brown, they happily ran around the kitchen, confidently exploring our shoelaces and everything they could get between their small, sharp baby teeth.

Caroline Fenton first came across this race in Australia while working there for a few months. She immediately fell in love with the animals. However, she does not believe that they are "better" than other shepherd dogs, she is just personally closer to them. By now she has even convinced her father, a breeder of award-winning Border collies, of the high quality of these Australians.

Kelpies, one of three Australian shepherd races, have been bred in their native land for almost a century. By now the International Dog Association has recognized these dogs as their own race. As working dogs about eighty thousand protect about 200 million sheep in Australia and New Zealand. Because of their intelligence and endurance they are increasingly appreciated by shepherds around the world. Kelpies are now used as sheep dogs in the United States, Canada, Kuwait, and Argentina, as well as in Hawaii, Kenya, and even the polar circle in Sweden, where the dogs' attention is devoted to the reindeer herds that can include up to twenty thousand animals. They are universal dogs who will not abandon their herd even under extreme circumstances such as burning hot sun, heavy snow, storms, and rain.

Their performances are impressive. We were convinced of this as we watched Caroline work with them: A sea of woolen backs rolls in front of one dog who keeps close to the end of the herd.

Immigration is too recent an event and the estancias of Patagonia are spread too far apart for one standard type of dog to have emerged in Patagonia. But one thing all these dogs have in common is their deeply rooted guarding instinct.

Suddenly the herd slows—an obstacle is blocking the way. Just like a gaucho hopping into the saddle, the dog jumps onto the closest sheep and from there quickly works its way to the front of the herd, stepping from back to back to restore order.

The dogs concentrate completely and demonstrate unbelievable enthusiasm. In comparison to the rather instinctive, rushing joy with which the Patagonian sheep dogs approach their work, the Australian dogs exhibit impressive form. The key to this difference is not to be found with the race, though; Caroline very deliberately adopted the complex training and discipline program of Australian dog trainers.

With about twenty commands she can exactly direct the dogs' every move: the dogs circle the herd clockwise or counterclockwise, freeze in their positions, slowly approach, or storm forward. Furthermore, Caroline can replace each command with a corresponding whistle, whistles that carry farther and influence the dogs more directly than the human voice.

The success of this perfect technique might be found in the dogs' ancient ancestors: the kelpies basically practice the hunting techniques of a pack of wolves. Among wolves the subordinate members of the pack circle the common prey and herd it toward the leader. Here in Patagonia, Caroline is the leader of the pack. But of course, she leaves out the last step, the

With three kelpies she brought from Australia, Caroline has established her own breed. This seven-week-old puppy is among the youngest addition to the dog family.

Until recently this would be a rare picture in Patagonia in every regard: a young woman, a motorcycle, and kelpies from Australia. Caroline Fenton has introduced the modern art of herding from the "mecca of sheep farmers."

killing of the prey.

The basics of their behavior have been passed down through generations of dogs for over fourteen thousand years. The selective breeding of working dogs by humans has accentuated certain aspects of their behavior. For example, with wolves the hunt is one process, but with the kelpies it is split into different parts. The kelpies have perfected what all shepherd dogs have: from their wolflike searching, discovering, approaching, and hunting comes the finding, ordering, threatening approach, and aimed driving. Selective breeding and training have eliminated other behavior patterns of the hunt: the grabbing, killing, and eating of the prey. If these instincts do break through in one of the dogs, this dog has to be removed from the pack. A herder dog that has taken to hunting Patagonian rabbits can no longer work with the sheep.

Above: Caroline's Kelpies know the fine art of the herder dogs. For Tango it is easy to run along the backs of sheep to clear a jam at the front of the herd.
Below: Kelpies are full of concentration when at work. They seem to direct the sheep using only their almost hypnotic gaze.

This has never happened among Caroline's dogs. Still, they don't give the impression of perfected working machines, but rather of lovable individuals—with equally lovable weak points. Tango, for example, Caroline's favorite dog, has a weakness for lambs. This can have negative effects out on the pasture. Determined, Tango looks for the smallest lamb in the herd and in complete fascination never lets it out of his sight—and in doing this he sometimes completely forgets about the rest of the herd. Only Caroline's commands bring him back into reality. Tango will only look at the lamb once more, and then he will continue to drive the herd forward. Many Australian sheep farmers ascribe much of the Border collie's and kelpie's effectiveness to their stare. It is said that it has an almost hypnotic effect on those they protect. Tango's actions confirmed this for us.

The Kelpie

Kelpies, medium-sized herder dogs from Australia, are increasingly favored by sheep farmers around the world. They have only been in Patagonia for the past few years where they are still rare. Their fur is short and smooth, either one color or with black, brown, reddish, or bluish gray spots.

The fur often exhibits red markings, which led to the false belief that Australian farmers had mixed domestic dingoes into the breeding begun over one hundred years ago. But there is no evidence to support this. Cynologists do believe it's possible that in the expanse of the outback—the Wild West of the fifth continent—there was occasional mixing between dingoes and kelpies. It is improbable, though, that this was done intentionally by humans since Australian sheep farmers hate dingoes as much as their colleagues in Patagonia hate the fox and puma.

The kelpies' primary ancestors are probably Scottish collies who were brought to Australia around 1860 and crossbred with other herder dogs. One of the first breeders, a farmer by the name of Gleason, is said to have traded a horse for a female dog from the already famous kennel of the Rutherford family. He named her Kelpie, which in Gaelic means "ghost of the water." He thereby coined the name for the slowly developing race since his kelpie, which was later called King's Kelpie, won the first shepherd dog competition in Australia in 1870.

Kelpies are extremely easy to care for with their short and weather-resistant fur. Yet they absolutely need to be kept outdoors and therefore they should not be kept as pets.

The Border Collie

Most of the dogs of Patagonian gauchos have at least some Border collie blood. In Great Britain and Ireland the Border collie has been the best-liked herder dog since the beginning of the century. The dog is smaller than a German shepherd, only a little taller than half a meter and weighing between fourteen and twenty-two kilograms. In the eighteenth century the Border collie began to be bred selectively, probably using a mix of domestic collies with continental dog races that arrived with sheep in the border region between England and Scotland. The dog's flexibility, endurance, and toughness, together with intelligence, quick learning skills, and, especially important for farmers, its unconditional obedience to precise whistle signals or called commands, caused its fame to spread far beyond the United Kingdom. Until the kelpie took its place the Border collie was considered "basic equipment" for an Australian sheep farmer. Characteristic of the Border collie is its crouched approach, the "hypnotic" gaze from its far-apart eyes, and its even temper. While the Border collie can be kept as a family dog, it needs to be constantly challenged with work or it will become grouchy and might even start to bite. Therefore, Border collies should only be kept with people willing to devote a lot of time to them.

Originally in England, but also throughout Europe and the United States, the Border collie has placed itself near the top of two other categories: agility, a type of dog sport, and obedience competitions. The Border collie has a rough, dense fur that forms a mane around its neck. The fur can be red, marbled blue, tricolored, black and white, brown, or black.

Tango is special not only as an excellent shepherd, but also as a potential father. The puppies we saw in the kitchen of the Fenton's descend from him. One of them accompanied us for one more day after we left Monte Dinero: for two hundred dollars—a steep sum considering that in Patagonia puppies are usually presented as gifts—Caroline sold the puppy to the family of a childhood friend. "I don't care about the money," said Caroline. "I just want to make sure that he is important to the new owners." Since we would be passing the friend's farm, which was about six hundred kilometers away, we gladly took the puppy and saved him from being sent by mail.

The drive took ten hours. Supporting our enthusiasm for the kelpies, our guest cried for his mother and his familiar surroundings for only about ten minutes before regaining composure and settling comfortably in the car. We actually would have liked to take him or one of his siblings back to Germany. But anyone who has seen the kelpies at work understands that this race can only lead a happy life when they also have a herd of sheep. And who could offer this back home?

The mountaintops of the Andes and the borderless expanse of Patagonia quicken the hearts of the adventurous.

GREENLAND

Companions in Ice and Snow

Give me winter, give me dogs—the rest you can keep!
Knud Johan Victor Rasmussen,
Across Arctic America, 1927

Previous page: In the fascinating and unforgiving environment of Greenland, dogs continue to be the most faithful companions for the hunters in their daily fight for survival.

The big white does not waste a single glance on the rambunctious pack behind him. Seemingly relaxed, he lies in the snow, his head on his paws, his tail lying still. Yet all his senses are concentrated on the feast that he awaits with unbelievable anticipation, it is about to begin.

His name is Nanok, the "polar bear." He is neither the biggest nor the strongest, but he is the smartest of Rasmus's sled dogs and thus the lead animal in the pack, which now, on shorter leashes behind him, demands its share of the loot with loud cries. Nanok does not have to do this: he can calmly observe Rasmus and hear the sound of the knife as it cuts through the already slightly frozen fish. He can let the salty smell waft in through his open nostrils. Above all, he can show dignity. Because of his longer leash Nanok is assured his own place to eat where he will not be disturbed; as the lead animal, the first chunk is his anyway. That is the tradition here in Greenland. And humans as well as dogs keep to these rituals because this—and only this—has proven to work best, especially for the lead animal whose position means not only duties, but also rights.

Rasmus now gets up. He cuts off the heads and tails of the two dozen fish, mostly halibut and a few codfish, and divides the rest into strips that are each about three fingers wide. He already gutted his catch at the ice

The fjords of Greenland have a large stock of fish. Across the frozen sea the fishermen in their dogsleds drive to the ice holes. Through these holes the long line—whose 150 hooks each need to have bait placed on them—is let down.

hole as soon as he brought up the net, before the fish could freeze. He throws Nanok an especially nice halibut head attached to a good piece of the especially fat back, and then the other dogs receive their share. But Rasmus only throws pieces to them too: feeding Greenland dogs by hand can be dangerous. A hungry pack of dogs does not differentiate between human fingers and fish.

Whoever catches a piece quickly swallows it. The dog who eats the fastest catches the most pieces. Rasmus does not interfere in the internal structure of the pack, so the stronger ones go first, while the lower-ranking animals have to pass at first and sometimes even give up a piece they already have caught. Rasmus sees to it that in the end everyone gets enough. To prevent biting on the next fishing expedition, all dogs have to have had equal amounts of food. In the winter they need one to two kilograms of high-quality food each day, but during the summer when food is more sparse, the portions are reduced to half a kilo since the dogs are "unemployed" in the summer. And, as the Greenlanders say, those who don't work shouldn't eat.

The puppies often receive seal innards in addition to the regular meat and fish. These contain all the nutrients dogs need to quickly grow into hard-working adults—which is the purpose of life for these dogs here in Greenland. Already the little ones demonstrate the originality of the race.

Greenlanders do not feed their dogs out of their hands. Fish or seal meat has to be thrown at the dogs because in their hunger the dogs would not discriminate between the fingers of the feeder and the meat.

Puppies often receive seal innards. The high concentration of vitamins and minerals contained in them is indispensable to the dogs' development.

When they hastily finish their bowls and look up with bloodied faces, they no longer look like little teddy bears but seem more like young wolves. This might possibly have a biological cause: the dogs of the world's largest island might be more closely related to wolves than any other race. The German zoologist Victor Goerttler described this in 1969: "The relatedness to the wolves is very apparent and finds expression in the independent character of the sled dogs as well. Even though they are products of breeding by humans, one cannot really consider these animals as pets. Aside from that, at intervals they are recrossed with wolves." Dog researcher Eberhard Trumler was certain of this as well: "We know from the Greenland dogs that up to recent times they have on occasion refreshed their genes with the wolves at home in Greenland *(Canis lupus orion)*." Today there are hardly any wolves left in Greenland. They are only in national parks where they rarely encounter dogs or humans.

Wolf blood or not, north of the polar circle, past the tree line, in the cold arctic steppe a dog race has emerged that, while exhibiting regional differences, overall corresponds to a common type. It is called the northland dog by zoologists. They believe, based on results of excavations, that it has a history of at least four thousand and possibly of as much as twelve thousand years.

Agreement, rare in cynology, exists on one point: humans must have brought these animals into the hostile environment of the far north. No domestic dog could have originated here, since wolves could not have joined humans at an evolutionary pace necessary for the human's survival.

It was only the dexterity, natural intelligence, stamina, and hardiness of dogs that enabled ancestors of today's Inuit, Indians, Lakotas, Lapps, Tschuktschen, and many other peoples around the world from Kamchatka to Greenland, Labrador to Alaska and the Aleutian Islands, to find new living spaces. Animals who could achieve this probably originated in eastern Asia. As companions on human expeditions they had to adapt to different environments. At some point they reached the far north of Eurasia and the Americas. The Russo-European Laika, northern Pomeranian, Japanese Shiba Inu, and Chinese Chow Chow represent some of their relatives who became sedentary on their world voyage. The Australian dingo is a descendant of a different strain of dogs. While the representatives of this strand also traveled with humans, they moved in the opposite direction. These animals who arrived in the north, we now call Siberian huskies, Alaskan malamutes, Samoyeds, Canadian Eskimo dogs, and Greenland dogs.

Eskimo dogs refers generally to all the races that are especially well suited as sled dogs. Geographically they are designated an area that is about seventy-five hundred kilometers long and twenty-five hundred kilometers wide. That is how large the living area is of the different peoples who we used to call Eskimos and who refer to themselves as Inuit, meaning "humans."

The white explorers and conquistadors did not see the Inuit as humans when they flocked toward the poles—especially the northern one—toward the end of the nineteenth century. They saw the natives as rabble. The famous Norwegian polar explorer Fridtjof Nansen disdainfully wrote in 1888: "The very hostile coast of Greenland that is only sparsely populated by heathen Eskimos is not a desirable place to spend the winter." In 1930 the German explorer Alfred Wegener complained in his diary: "The Greenlander does not think more than two minutes ahead: the Germans will know what to do."

The dogs of the Inuits were not much loved by some of the explorers either. German naturalist Georg Wilhelm Steller (1709–1746) scornfully noted about his aides: "The dogs are very shy. They have no love for or loyalty to their master. One has to use tricks to harness them in front of the sled." And Fridtjof Nansen wrote about the animals who saved his life several times during his expeditions: "Rascals: not a day passes without a fight. There is not a sense of nobility in the dogs." Nansen continued to use the dogs though; most explorers and adventurers in reality knew all too well the value of dogs in the ever expansive ice.

Only one explorer wanted to do without them entirely. Against all warnings Robert Falcon Scott wanted to win the race for the discovery of the South Pole with motor sledges and ponies. "One pony does the work of at least ten dogs," Scott said—an incorrect calculation that he and all the members of his expedition paid for with their lives. The motor sledges quickly broke down and the ponies froze in their own sweat. At last the humans lost in their fight against the desert of ice. When the victor of the race, Roald Amundsen, was asked about the reasons for his success and Scott's catastrophe, he replied, "We had dogs—they didn't."

We had been warned about the dogs: Greenland dogs are wild and aggressive; they would even kill children if they were lying on the ground in a seal-like position. But what we observed was the contrary. Even small children play with the sled dogs of the family—not only with the puppies, but also with full-grown dogs. We did not see a single attack—only displays of friendly and almost enthusiastic canine devotion when the dogs received attention.

Of course Greenland dogs aren't cuddly pets in our sense of the word.

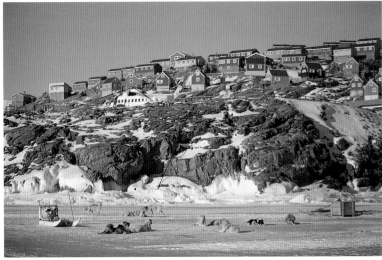

For over seven months of the year, the sea around Uummannaq is frozen. Winter is the time of the sled dogs. The harnesses are tied up directly on the ice and the dogs are always ready for their next mission.

Humans who have to survive in such a hostile environment cannot afford such a luxury. The dogs are intended solely to make survival for humans in this environment possible. For this they are respected, loved, bred—not for appearance, as is the standard in the industrialized world, but for performance. This, along with animal prey, is the only life insurance that northern peoples have. The dogs are their companions and they are exposed to the same conditions as humans. Here the interdependence that must have existed at the beginning of the bond between humans and dogs is still evident: by both species living together, they, in the pursuit of their own endeavors, benefit each other.

For those not familiar with the land this might appear cruel, or it might be misinterpreted as the Inuit not caring for their animals. In reality, however, the Inuit have a relationship with their dogs that over millennia has proved to work for both dog and master. Rasmus, the fisher and hunter, provides a good example of this.

Rasmus lives in Uummannaq, a real city by Greenland standards with a population of about thirteen hundred on an island with the same name at about 70° northern latitude. This region boasts the thickest sea ice in the world and for more than seven months of the year the fishing boats are anchored in the frozen harbor. During this period the dogsleds have to do the hardest work. The temperature sometimes drops to fifty degrees below zero (Celsius).

In April, it was still twenty degrees below zero, which because of the dry air is easily bearable by the people in their warm seal and polar bear furs and by the dogs who are already starting to shed their winter fur. Even

Greenland dogs are favorite playmates of the children. One often sees youngsters carry around puppies the way children in the West carry dolls or teddy bears. In this way, humans as well as dogs learn how to interact with each other from the start.

the puppies have to adapt to these temperatures. Like everywhere in Greenland, the dogs live outside from birth, protected only a little from wind and weather by a small wooden shelter. The animals need to get used to the hard living conditions from the start; otherwise later on they will not be able to fulfill their duties. If a puppy dies from this first hurdle in life it would not have survived the much greater strains that are to follow—natural selection in its original form. Over millennia this has given the Greenland dogs their hardiness.

Only in their first six months do Rasmus's dogs have freedom: they are allowed to play, especially with the children, who carry them in their arms as children in our homes carry dolls or teddy bears. But soon the little

Greenland

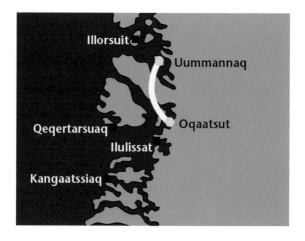

With its 2.2 million square kilometers, the largest island in the world is about fifty times the size of its mother country, Denmark. Greenland stretches between the sixtieth and eighty-third degrees of northern latitude before the eastern coast of North America. Over 80 percent of the area is covered year round by a solid sheet of ice that can be up to thirty-two hundred meters thick. Statisticians have calculated that the level of the world's oceans would rise by six meters if a change in climate caused this mass of ice to melt.

A slightly more advantageous climate seems to have prevailed in this region in 982 B.C. when the Viking Erik the Red became the first European to discover the island; he named it Green Land. However, he did not come entirely voluntarily. Because he had killed a man in Iceland he was declared "free to be killed" for three years and had to leave the country. His family lived in Iceland in the first place only because his father had been forced to leave Norway for the very same reason. When Erik the Red had waited out his three-year sentence he only returned to Iceland to lure more settlers to his new island. In 985, an armada of twenty-five ships set sail for Greenland, but only fourteen of those actually reached their destination. On the south of the island the Vikings founded a permanent colony. Was it epidemic, a negative change in climate, or—but less likely—a fight with the northern Inuit that led to the sudden disappearance of the Viking colony from Greenland about four hundred years later? The answer remains a puzzle to this day.

The next Europeans only reached the "green island" centuries later. In the seventeenth and eighteenth centuries whale hunters were the island's primary visitors. The whale oil extracted from the fat of whales acted as fuel for Europe's lamps, serving a similar function as oil today. But explorers and adventurers were also increasingly attracted to the island. In 1888 the Norwegian Fridtjof Nansen became the first to cross the inland ice of Greenland. In 1931 during an attempt to research the mass of ice throughout the year and to spend the winter in the midst of the ice, the highly regarded German polar scientist Alfred Wegener died. The most famous son of Greenland, Knud Rasmussen, also should be listed among the exceptional explorers of Greenland.

In the eighteenth century the Danes opened trading posts along the west coast that were eventually consolidated to the company KGH (Kongelige Gronlandske Handel), which held the monopoly on trade until 1950. In this way Greenland became a Danish colony, and in 1953 it became an integrated part of the Danish empire. However, since 1979 this island has been under its own administration.

Of particular economic significance in the past was the mining of cryolite, a rare mineral needed for aluminum production. But cryolite supplies are now depleted, and the mining of further natural resources is hardly profitable because of the climatic conditions not to mention that it is dangerous to the sensitive arctic environment. Since the 1950s Denmark has offered substantial subsidies each year to Greenland residents. Today sheep and reindeer farming are a source of income for Greenland's fifty-five thousand inhabitants, but fishing on the island's very rewarding fishing grounds is the population's main occupation. There are canneries throughout the country and Greenland further increases revenues by selling fishing rights to the European Union. Families of the hunters and fishermen are self-sufficient through seal hunting and fishing.

puppies start pulling toy sleds and in a playful manner are introduced to the commands they will hear their entire lives: *illi-li illi-li*, "go right," *iu iu*, "go left," *jiup jiup*, "faster," and *ai ai*, "stop."

The nicest command is *dama*, "let's go!" At this Rasmus's sled is pulled by fifteen adult dogs across fields of snow and blocks of ice that are pressed together. The dogs spread out like a fan in front of him. The fan is one of two harness formations. It is the one typical for Greenland since there are no trees in the way of the team. For Greenland teams the major risk is that the ice might break as the dogs run across. But in the fan formation, an injured dog does not pull the other ones down, and the driver can save him by pulling on just the injured dog's leash. In deep snow the fan has the disadvantage of each dog having to plow its own lane, but fields of soft snow are rare in Greenland. With the second harness method, the feather, dogs are tied to the left and right of a leading leash. This method is used in forests or in terrain with obstacles or narrow paths—conditions that prevail, for example, in arctic North America. Here near Uummannaq the animals can always run in the broad fan formation.

In about eleven hours we traveled 120 kilometers with Rasmus. We accompanied him to see his father Jonas in Illorsuit. Nanok the Polar Bear led Rasmus's pack; behind him, the strongest animals ran in the middle and the weaker ones ran at the sides. At the start the dogs were fast and seemed to have boundless energy. But after a while their tongues hung out, their speed decreased a little, and the animals slowed to their usual trot.

During a journey Rasmus keeps an eye on all the animals as well as the surroundings. If he wants to change direction he reaches for the dog whip,

The sled leader steers his team with different commands. *Dama,* "let's go," is the command the dogs like to hear most.

which is about sixty centimeters long—it is fitted to the length of the driver's arm—and has a five-meter-long seal-leather strap attached to it. When he needs to Rasmus can hit each dog very precisely with the whip. Most of the time he only uses this extended arm to keep the attention of the pack or to direct it to the desired direction. Nonetheless, the animals have great respect for it. A couple of times on the trip the dogs stop to rest—the dogs themselves decide when. During the rest they get some chunks of pemmican, dry food. The pack quenches its thirst on the way by eating snow as they run.

When we arrived in Illorsuit Rasmus cared for his dogs even before greeting his family. He carefully checked for sores on the dogs' paws caused by the sharp edges of the ice and for snow clumped between their toes. Only then was there a short exchange between father and son. Greenlanders do not carry their hearts on their sleeves; feelings are expressed more through small gestures than through big words. It is telling that the first conversation between Rasmus and Jonas revolved around the dogs. Filled with pride, the older man showed us the next generation of his animals. Soon after that we met his adult animals too when Jonas took us all to the seal hunt.

Sometimes the hunt for one of the six types of animals that live in the waters around Greenland still takes place using a harpoon, spear, or nets, but most of the time a shotgun is used. In contrast to the fishnets that drift deep along the bottom of the sea, the seal nets hang directly under the ice. They are small and are set out close to breathing holes.

Breathing holes are just small enough for a seal to slip through for a

The crying of the sled dogs never stops in the settlements. At the slightest provocation one of the dogs will start the concert.

The dogs love their work in the harness. With each drive they loudly beg to come along. Most of the time one or several dogs with slightly longer leashes lead the team.

short nap on the ice—and often the holes are covered by drifting snow. Jonas knows the breathing holes, but the dogs, too, can find them in this great white expanse without his help, and without training. They have proved themselves to be hunting companions as well.

To Greenlanders, seals are among the most important game. During the summer whales are added to this list. Polar bears, too, are hunted, but they live primarily in the north and east. Musk oxen are found only in the south, as are reindeer, which were reimported to the island from Scandinavia after they had been hunted to extinction. The departure of fish and seals from the coastal waters (because of changes in the water temperature of less than one degree Celsius) has always been a problem in Greenland and has in the past led to many food shortages. In recent years, fishing has almost overtaken the seal hunt in significance because the fish can also be sold to small canneries that have been established throughout the country by Danish trading companies. As a "by-product" sharks are often pulled up in the nets or on the hooks.

One cannot afford to waste anything here. Even the somewhat undesirable ice or Greenland shark (*Somniosus microcephalus*) is used—but only as food for the dogs. While after proper treatment the meat of the Greenland shark is not harmful to humans, it does not taste good. This may be because of the high urea content in the shark's tissue. Through changing the salt concentration in its body the shark can adapt to the various electrolytic

Eskimos: the Inuit

The ancestors of the Inuit came from Asia, probably from Mongolia, walking in several waves to North America. Today it has been established that the water level was so low twelve thousand years ago that a dry bridge existed across the Bering Strait. The reason for this movement is unclear, but tribal rivalries might have played a role. In searching for a new place to live, single groups in different periods walked all the way to Greenland. It has been proved that the Saqqaq group that settled Greenland, probably around 2000 B.C., kept dogs whose skeletal bones closely resemble today's sled dogs. However, these peoples did not survive in Greenland; they died because of changes in the climate. The ancestors of today's Greenlanders arrived on the island before A.D. 1000.

Until his death in 1933, the Greenland researcher Knud Rasmussen tirelessly traveled on his dogsled among the Inuit in Greenland, the North American arctic, and Siberia. By doing this he traveled, in reverse order, the initial route of Inuit migration and was the first to prove that they are indeed related to one another and speak, in only slightly varying dialects, the same language.

Western civilization assigned them the name Eskimo, an Indian word that white people adopted early in the nineteenth century from the Cree in Canada, one of the about twenty tribes of North American Algonquin Indians. In the Cree's language, *escee* means "unbearable" and *mau* means "humans."

The Cree found it unbearable that this people that bordered on their territory ate raw meat. This is how in other Algonquin dialects terms such as *wiyaskimowok*, meaning "eaters of raw meat," came about. The so-called Eskimos refer to themselves as Inuit, or "humans." They looked down on their neighbors whom they considered less worthy. For a long time they found the term Eskimo to be derogatory. However, with newfound consciousness of their ethnic identity they now stand by the fact that the consumption of raw meat and fish is an important part of their culture and they for the most part accept—sometimes even with a certain pride—the name Eskimo.

In contrast to other Inuit peoples, Greenlanders are Christian—a result of missionary trips that started in the Middle Ages. In the seventeenth century, when whale hunters came to Greenland, the Greenland Inuit and the Europeans mixed. To this day many Inuit carry European names.

Because of the growing influence of industry the traditional lifestyle of the Inuit has changed and the ethnic identity of this hunter peoples is endangered. But thanks to the careful policy of Denmark, this is taking place to a lesser degree in Greenland than in North America, for example, or in the former Soviet Union.

conditions in its different hunting territories, be it just below the surface of the ocean or several hundred meters deep. Because of this, the shark's meat cannot be consumed by dogs when fresh; fresh shark meat affects them like alcohol and can at times even be lethal. Only meat that has been dried for at least six months can be fed to the dogs. But, according to an August 20, 1930, diary entry by the Greenland explorer Alfred Wegener even "well-dried shark meat is dangerous. The dogs get cramps after eating it; especially when they are thin, they cannot handle more than one small chunk a day." (Wegener made these observations in the Disko bay on his last journey. He died a little over a year later about three hundred kilometers away from Uummannaq in the inland ice.)

Jonas and Rasmus, on the other hand, can feed their generally well-fed dogs during times when food is scarce, or in the summer when the dogs are not working, with the prepared shark meat and can thereby keep the desired seal meat for themselves and their families. Seal meat contains the minerals necessary for the human organism, as well as necessary vitamins, which are especially plentiful in the seal's liver. Thus seal meat constitutes an important source of nutrients since vegetables are a rare, imported luxury in Greenland. In the short summer months no more than a few radishes and occasionally some broccoli grow in the small gardens. It is mostly European immigrants who stubbornly—and often unsuccessfully—try to obtain something from nature that nature did not intend for this area.

The hunt and what is caught continue to determine the menu and daily lives of humans and dogs as they have for millennia, especially in the

For cooperation in the harness a hierarchy in the pack is necessary. With fights or demeaning gestures this social order is constantly reaffirmed.

small settlements north of the polar circle. For his pack of fifteen dogs alone during the work-intensive season Jonas needs about twenty-five kilograms of meat or fish each day—about three pounds per animal. Only with his sled can he procure the amount of food he needs for his family and his dogs. If he is lucky he can get several hundred kilos in one catch. On the return trip the dogs then have to pull more than thirty kilograms each.

The climate, the hard living conditions, the daily hunt, the long dark winters, and the short summers have shaped not only the relationship between human and dog, but also human societal structures. As opposed to the situation for the Inuit of Canada, Alaska, and the former Soviet Union, here the Inuit are still largely intact. Even though growing industries have changed much in Uummannaq, Greenlanders have not lost their ethnic identity to the same degree as other small cultures. They have not yet entirely sacrificed their culture on the altar of modernization. They still live with their dogs while other Inuit now almost exclusively use snowmobiles. Alcohol does not play the role here that vodka and whiskey played in the pauperization of the Inuit of North America and Russia, even though here, too, stories of alcohol-related tragedies are heard from time to time,

Already as puppies the animals begin to build a hierarchy through play.

The Greenland Dog

The strong, enduring dogs of the Inuit in Greenland have found fans in other parts of the world, and because of this they are bred, along with Alaskan malamutes, Siberian huskies, and Samoyeds, outside of their original habitat as their own race. In Switzerland they helped transport food and mail during the expansion of the rack railway to the Jungfraujoch in 1912. However, the Swiss made a mistake by placing some newly arrived Greenland dogs into a common kennel with Samoyeds. Only the Greenland dogs survived the fights that ensued.

The animals mostly stay in their region and only rarely show signs of crossbreeding with other races. The most important reason for this is a law that limits the keeping of sled dogs to the area past the polar circle. This is why the polar circle is also called the dog equator in Greenland: no sled dog is allowed to cross it southward (the only exception is for the geographically isolated hunter community Ammassalik in eastern Greenland), and no other dogs are allowed to enter. Mixtures with other races are therefore largely prevented. Thus, when these strong polar dogs were recognized in 1967 by the International Purebred Dog Federation (FCI) as an independent breed, they were already a completely stable race.

Greenland dogs are bred for the long and hard work of being sled dogs. They are also useful as hunting companions. However, they cannot be used as guard dogs: these animals are very accustomed to humans and have never developed guarding instincts.

After one has experienced how important an uninhibited pack dynamic is to humans and their special work with the dogs, the following comment made by the German wildlife biologist Wolfgang Schröder in a recent TV interview is understandable: "The last thing I want to be is a dog among the Eskimos." Schröder was referring to the dogs who are kept on leashes and chains that do not allow for dogs to run around freely. But we experienced this differently in Greenland: the free running that Greenland dogs need and yearn for is their work in the harness.

especially from the area farther north around Thule where the United States keeps their listening post in the arctic on a massive military base.

In Illorsuit, the settlement where Jonas lives, we encountered a curious sight: even the voluntary firefighters get to a fire via dogsled—complete with hoses, sirens, and flashing lights. Whoever has just put their dogs into harness and hears the sirens has to immediately make their dogs available to the firefighters and for the time being postpone their hunting expedition.

Be it on duty for a fire call or on a joyride to the seal hunt: for the dogs, each run in front of the sled is eagerly and impatiently anticipated. The animals probably understand each fan formation on their leashes with the lead animal in front as the beginning of a hunt—as their ancient wolf instinct tells them. To keep this instinct alive, humans never interfere in the hierarchical fights that occur regularly in a pack.

During these fights there can be serious biting that sometimes results in major injuries. Jonas, like many Greenlanders, tries to prevent the damage in advance. With sharp pliers he takes off the points of the dogs' sharp teeth when they are still young. This capping is only necessary once in a dog's life, and the dogs quickly forget this painful procedure. After this, if there is a fight in the pack, the shortened teeth can only barely penetrate through the fur of the opponent. This capping has proved itself a valuable protection for the dogs from their own social rules.

These rules are relatively strict because when the animals are in the harness or taking rests they cannot avoid one another. And after their first half year, the dogs, as is common among almost all working Inuit dogs, live their lives on the leash. In Greenland it is even a law that after six months of age dogs have to be on a leash. The only exceptions are mothers with their puppies. Rasmus explained the reason for this: keeping dogs on leashes is the only way to prevent rabies and other diseases from spreading from wild polar foxes to the dogs. In the winter of 1987–88 an illness killed almost all the dogs in Thule and the hunters were dependent on welfare until, after a pledge throughout the country, hundreds of healthy dogs from other districts were flown in on helicopters.

But another deciding factor is that only leashed dogs are always immediately ready for humans. If the dogs roamed about freely they would constantly have to be searched and called for, or even caught. Their training would be more difficult. Also, the risk that one of the valuable dogs would be killed by a polar bear would increase considerably.

The dogs have gotten used to this life over thousands of generations and do not suffer from it because the external conditions of their lives with humans have long since been incorporated into their inherited be-havioral patterns. "Freely" kept Greenland dogs quickly lose a typical char-acteristic of their race: the social behavior that secures their place in the hierarchical structure so important for their work in the pack. They are not used to the rules their free-running counterparts have in their lives with humans. Greenland dogs can react unpredictably, even aggressively, to these rules.

Among the dogs of Rasmus and his father, Jonas, we observed neither unpredictable behavior nor aggression. Instead the animals helped us imag-ine the experiences of the Greenlander Knud Rasmussen: "We labored together like only beings that live together could, at times against the impassable pack ice, at times in the rush of the hunt, but always happiest when we were already cramped up from hunger and longing for meat and were able to see the settlement in a distance."

The significance the dog has had for many peoples' development is evident in Greenland to this day. In spite of all their skills, without the adaptability and stamina of their dogs the Inuit could never have made the polar world their habitat. Greenland was and continues to be a rough and hostile country, but it's also a fascinating challenge for humans and their most faithful helper and companion: the dog.

NAMIBIA

The Dogs of the Red Herders

With a glowing thunder Ndjambi Karunghe, the creator of all things, once upon a time sent a dog to the humans. Since then in their camps, Okuruwo, the holy fire, has always burned and the dogs, as a reward, are allowed to sleep next to their ashes.
MYTH OF THE HIMBA

When Wahenuna steps outside his hut in the mornings, his day begins with a ritual: the personal greeting of his most important four-legged companions. Wahenuna is the most influential man of the kraals because he owns the most cattle. But his first steps lead him to his two dogs. They carry meaningful names: Hakoquoko, the darker one, reminds the human, "Hold him at your hand," and Metunai, the lighter of the two, promises, "I will die with you." In a country in which every trace in the sand can signify good or bad luck, names are more than just sounds—they are messages from the world of the gods and ancestors.

Kaokoveld is the name of this country in the far northeast of Namibia. Semidesert, desert, and dry savannas are all found here where the sun mercilessly beats on the earth. Shadows are cast only by the occasional bushy mopane tree. Water is found only in a few rivers and also in mud holes during the rainy season; the only other source of water is wells dug deep into the red earth. For humans and animals this means they must be satisfied with the little that this hostile land is willing to give.

The Himba have perfected this way of life. Traditions, rituals, and social behavior have evolved over thousands of years so that everything is secondary to the goal of survival, even the beauty regimens that turn the already well-formed, noble-faced people into spectacular apparitions.

Ruaquahirua and her sister Uawethako, two of Wahenuna's neighbors, initiate us to these regimens. The two women grind up ironstone, a red mineral containing iron oxide, and mix the fine powder with milk fat and herbs to create a salve they apply to their hair, faces, and bodies. Their glowing color, which slowly rubs off on most of their commonly used objects, explains why these people are also called the red herders. This makeup ritual does not grow solely from an aesthetic desire of the Himba, but also stems from a practical nature: the red cream protects the skin from the sun and insect bites. While the result is spectacular, the method is simple. This is typical for these people, of whom only around four to five thousand live in the Namibian Kaokoveld, with another three

Previous page: The Kaokoveld in far northwest Namibia is the territory of the Himba. The beauty of the landscape hides the fact that it is very hard for the Himba to lead their herder lives there.

thousand residing on the other side of the northern border in Angola.

The animals they have reflect their practicality and their focus on preserving traditions: cows, cattle, and sangas (a mixture of zebus and shorthorn cattle), a few sheep, many goats, and their dogs, who on their travels and in the kraal have many responsibilities. The cows provide the milk, one of the most important sources of food for the people. The meat consumed by the Himba usually comes from the goats and sheep. Only rarely are cattle slaughtered, and then it is for festivities. The cattle are part of the religious life of the Himba, and like ancestors, they are considered to be the donors of energy for life, and even life itself. Owning cattle signals power and gains one respect. The dogs' main responsibility is to protect the cattle who are out on the free pasture during the day and in the cattle pens in the middle of the kraal at night.

That the dogs are able to handle this responsibility seems strange at first, so withdrawn and unspectacular do they appear at first sight. Cynologists used to classify them as pariah dogs, raceless dogs who procreate without specific breeding and and live like vagabonds in the belt of warm and temperate zones around the globe. This negative description, which is based on human bias, caused protests early on. In 1904, Richard Strebel, a German cynologist, asserted that "zoologists exhibit a

Wahenuna is the most influential man in his Himba village, and his dog Metunai is always at his side. The dog's name indicates a close relationship: *Metunai* translates as "I will die with you."

In the religious beliefs of the Himba cattle are the donors of life energy and life in general. Their milk also provides the Himba's main source of nutrition. The cattle have to be protected against hyenas, leopards, and lions—which is only one of the dogs' many important responsibilities.

very stepmother-like behavior toward this dog." His colleague Ludwig Beckman had given a different opinion ten years earlier. He found it "incomprehensible that even in recent times the pariah dogs of different countries have been subjected to careful scrutiny of skull and skeleton in the hopes to gain by these means information about the ancestors of the house dog."

Yet it was exactly this that the Austrian dog scientist Emil Hauck demanded again in the 1940s, because he believed he would be able to find "original blood" in these dogs, from which the different races of dogs descended. Along with the term *pariah dog,* which originated in England, the term *schensi dog* appeared, introduced in 1949 by the German zoologist Erich Werth in his confused discussion of pariah and purebred dogs. Schensi dogs to him were "mostly in the first stages of domestication that appear especially in tropical countries"; they were "primitive dogs of the tropical hoe-culture belt that survive without human assistance but live in and around human settlements."

This discussion about dogs becomes more understandable when one considers the much more heated discussions that took place at the same time about so-called primitive peoples. By denigrating the dogs the cynologists were actually commenting on the dogs' owners. We met both—humans and dogs—in distant Namibia, and neither deserve to be judged by the eyes of our civilization as primitives nor as pariahs.

In reality a mutually beneficial relationship between human and animal has developed here. It is not apparent at first sight, but we repeatedly observed how great the reciprocal dependence and respect is. A hint of this lies in the Himba's tradition of only giving significant names to humans and dogs. Goats and sheep, although highly valued as livestock and treated well, remain nameless.

When there is slaughtering in a Himba kraal the dogs get the leftovers. They thereby actually fulfill an important hygienic function around the huts. Yet in addition to getting scraps they are also pur-

posely fed. They often get sour milk mixed with corn porridge, since the Himba start cultivating the earth close to their kraal during longer sedentary periods. It was near one of their fields where we started talking with a Himba woman who was visiting our camp with her two daughters.

She had found a grenade, a relic from the SWAPO's (South West Africa People's Organization) fight for independence against the South African army that took place even here in the remote territory of the Himba. We suggested that she report her finding to the police as numerous posters that are posted everywhere in the small towns and trading posts suggest. We inquired whether she at least had dogs with her for protection. She shook her head. Dogs belong almost exclusively to men. Only rarely do they trust women with dogs. More commonly they are given to children— as protectors. The two girls, however, did not yet have one; they are eagerly anticipating the day their father will give them a guard dog.

"I already have a name for my dog," said the older girl. "Dieb will be its name."

"Why?" I asked.

"I don't know, that's just what I thought of. You don't think Dieb is a good name?" She was maybe six years old, and we did not want to disappoint her. So we agreed with her that Dieb would be a great name for a dog. "Oh well," she replied, "maybe I will name him something else, too. What do you call your dogs?" We listed a few typical names. "And how much cattle do you have?" We admitted we had none, and the girl was surprised. No cattle? But dogs? What for? "You guys have strange dogs."

Often the natural and relaxed relationship between humans and dogs among ancient peoples like the Himba is misinterpreted as carelessness. However, the Himba's dogs are respected individuals; all have an owner and their own name.

Like cattle, among the Himba dogs are the property of the men. But in almost every kraal there are also dogs who protect and accompany the children and women.

Namibia

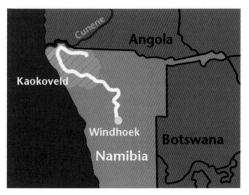

Namibia is twice the size of Germany, stretching through southwestern Africa. Apart from its coastline it is a highland, areas inland lying up to eighteen hundred meters above sea level. Only three border rivers carry water throughout the entire year: in the south the Orange and in the north the Kunene and the Okavango. Apart from its subtropical northwest, Namibia has a dry, almost desert climate throughout the year, with summer temperatures (November to March) reaching forty degrees Celsius.

Namibia has among the lowest population density in the world. Its 1.5 million inhabitants belong to different ethnic groups (Ovambo, Herero, Damara, Bushmen, Nama, and others), each of whom speaks a different language. For this reason the official language is English and the common second language is Afrikaans. However, in Windhoek, the capital, and in many other places, communication is also possible in German (Germany colonized the southwestern area of Namibia).

Namibians mainly live off agriculture—cattle farming in the north, sheep farming in the south. The country is rich in—only partially exploited—natural resources (such as diamonds, gold, uranium oxide) that aside from the rapidly growing tourist industry present an important revenue. Namibia only became independent (from the Republic of South Africa) in 1990. In spite of many tribal and national differences the young state is today considered the prime example of African democracy.

The Himba have a clear division of labor that includes dogs. They are usually needed on the grazing grounds to deter wild animals—lions, hyenas, and leopards are always attracted by herds. Out in the bush the cattle are guarded mostly by the men, the goats by the children, with most of the dogs at their side. The remaining ones stay at the huts or accompany the women. But the dogs, just like the cattle, are the property of the men.

Even though the Himba are often used as an example of a matriarchal society, this is not entirely accurate. It would be more appropriate to classify them as a matrilineal society: seven *eanda*, or matrilineal clans, each of which is traced back to a common tribal mother, determine the origins of all Himba. Their societal importance, which regulates, for example, inheritance, outweighs the existing twenty *oruzo*, or partrilineal clans. A son, for example, does not inherit the cattle of his father, but rather that of his mother's brother. This emphasis on the maternal line and the material benefits of the marriages has a simple, practical use: the pattern of inheritance prevents inbreeding among the cattle, because the inheriting family almost always lives in a different kraal.

The encounter with the mother and her daughters led us to their kraal the next day. There we could closely observe the division of labor among the humans and among the dogs. The head of the family in this kraal is Mauru. His favorite dog Ondangar is always near him.

The big male Ondangar is Mauru's favorite dog. He proudly accompanies his master on his daily patrol rounds.

The animal often accompanies his master, especially on the long walks through the steppe. There Mauru looks for poachers who, in the name of the Namibian agency for wildlife protection, are hunting for trophies or simply meat. Hunting, for whatever reason, seems to go against the Himba's beliefs. They recognize the right to life of all the animals in their territory and are ready to defend this.

These people, who in the sixteenth century immigrated to the area at the lower Kuene (today's southern Angola and northern Namibia), have no hunting traditions, but they have always kept cattle. The Himba believe in a balance in nature. Even if on occasion a goat or even cattle are killed by an animal, they do not start out on a hunt for revenge. There's no reason to go after hyenas or lions because evil spirits, in their eyes, are responsible for such a loss. Only defending the herd is allowed. We observe how Mauru teaches his sons how to use a club to drive away thieves from the herds, for only later, when they have proved that they are ready to face the dangers in the bush on their own, will they have earned the spears of men and the possession of their own dogs.

Ondangar is not Mauru's only dog. Mauru owns several dogs and all fulfill tasks that seem to suit their character perfectly. Okandono, for example, loves to be away with the cattle. She knows her task so well that without command she comes along when the cattle go into the bush. The dog Babille is entirely different: she prefers the presence of the women in the camp. This is not only because the good-tasting sour milk is prepared here: she also stays at their side if a hut needs to be renovated or when the women go into the bush to collect wood. The women welcome this—less

out of a fear of animals, who usually avoid humans, but more out of a fear of snakes. Snakes can lie invisible in the high grass and easily bite a careless walker. Babille reliably warns them of this danger—doing so out of instinct, since nobody ever taught her this.

Just as Babille stays with the women, the young Tahanau takes care of the children. Playfully the dog is taught this responsibility. At first she accompanies her human playmates on their search for mopane worms, which are a change in the diet of the Himba. In this season the worms are plentiful and the children collect them in mopane bushes. They then roast them over the fire and let them dry in the sun for a few days before eating them. Tahanau tackles this challenge with visible joy and of her own volition. She seems to believe she's the worm dog of the village. Through her participation in the search for worms, she becomes more of a protector for the children. This side benefit seems to have developed completely naturally and without any prompting by

Babille always stays close to the women, even if they go out into the bush to look for wood. Many times she has warned of snakes that were hidden in the grass at the women's feet.

humans. The Himba never force a particular responsibility onto a dog; the dog chooses its own.

After these observations we must correct the statements of our friend from the cornfield: it is true that these dogs mostly belong to the men, but it is not rare for them to be left with the women and children in whose lives they are completely integrated. Reports from many parts of the world about lager, schensi, pariah, and guard dogs contain similar observations: women and dogs among people living in "primitive" lifestyles seem to constitute a natural unit, as long as they are in a hunter-gatherer society. In contrast to this, in hunting communities the stronger master-dog relationship seems to have developed, a relationship that is found in most industrialized countries as well. Based on this observation, the wolf and dog scientist Erik Zimen developed a theory about domestication in which it is possible that young

The Himba

The Himba belong to the Bantu people who are part of the Herero tribe and live in the far northwestern part of Namibia. Their territory, the so-called Kaokoveld, borders Angola. It is believed these people of about eight thousand immigrated in the sixteenth century from what is today Ethiopia and Kenya.

A protective fence several miles long that the white farmers in Namibia erected to protect their cattle from plague guaranteed the Himba a relative isolation and safety for a long time. Only the warring conflicts of the past decades—the arrival of the South African army during the fight for independence and the war in Angola and its spread across the border—led to closer contact with civilization.

Today the kraals of the Himba are a favorite destination for tourists, and this contact with the outside world is fast destroying the traditional world of this people. Ethnologists assume that only Himba who are adults today will complete their lives in the old social structures. Along with the Massai in Kenya and the Wodaabe in the Sahel, the Himba belong to the last traditional herder peoples of today's black Africa.

But unlike them, the Himba are doubly threatened: the Namibian government is planning an immense dam at the Epupa Falls on the Kunene River. The Epupa valley, a central part of the Himba territory, would be flooded by the dam. At the present time, international protests have been able to stop the project, but it is not off the agenda yet.

As among all old Bantu peoples, the celebration of ancestors plays a central role in the Himba's religious beliefs. However, their thoughts and feelings revolve mostly around their cattle. The cattle are also the focal point of religious beliefs. In symbolic form the attributes of these animals, such as their horns, are integrated into the jewelry and head and hair decorations of women. The cattle pen always forms the center of the kraal. The duration of the stay in the kraal is determined by the grazing needs of the herds. If the herds no longer find enough to eat around the village, the kraal is left. The village community leaves the huts until the area's environment has had a chance to regenerate. One problematic aspect of this is keeping the goats along with the cattle, since the goats permanently damage the pastures.

wolf puppies at some point in the Stone Age were taken by humans of different tribes to their camps. They needed milk, "yet that of goat, sheep, and cattle was not available at that time. Only women were able to provide the puppies with the necessary nutrition." Zimen concludes: "According to the Bible it was not Adam but Eve whose actions led to expulsion from paradise, and actions not born of need, but curiosity. Could it be that our civilization, which has been accompanied and made possible in part by domesticated dogs, began with the unintentional taming of a few wolf puppies by a woman?"

Each dog seems to find its own set of tasks without guidance from humans. For example, nobody gave Mekoronai commands or taught her to accompany the cows, but she still goes wherever they go.

Among a different African tribe, the Turkana in east Africa, who live similarly to the Himba, Zimen encountered certain patterns of behavior that influence the division of labor. As among the Himba, dogs among the Turkana fulfill the role of the babysitter, often remaining with infants and small children to guard them while their mothers are busy with other tasks. Dogs also keep the camp clean by eating baby feces. The Turkana's dogs even lick the children clean; Zimen speaks of "diaper substitution." We too found the dogs of the Himba to be a kind of voluntary and independent garbage collector.

It remains a mystery from whom these dogs descend. It is hard to imagine that under the often light yellow, occasionally red-brown, and the rare black-white furs, there is only the genes of the father of all dogs, the wolf. At least in Europe there seems to be no scientific doubt, even though researchers such as American Michael Fox see in the pariah and schensi dogs a transition form that might be the connecting link between the extinct original dog and today's dogs. But for most scientists, such theories belong to the realm of fairy tales. These scientists reject the assumption that some long-extinct original dogs, who are supposed to have existed along with or even before the wolf in prehistoric times, could be the ancestors for the many different dog races of the world. They also reject the hypothesis that jackals participated in the creation of dogs. While most scientists believe a crossing between jackals and dogs is possible, they cannot explain the surprising similarity of the dogs among the Himba and other tribes not only in Africa, but also in Asia. Probably the hard and relatively similar climates at different places on Earth caused, independent of one another, comparable biological and character adaptations. Only in Israel has a recognized race evolved out of this: the Israeli Canaan dog.

The clearest definition of the Himba's dogs that is also scientifically useful has been developed by the Menzels, a German-Israeli couple who has worked with these dogs for over thirty years. The pariahs are in no way "raceless" mixtures; on the contrary, they are widespread members of a natural race that without human interference has remained surprisingly pure in many parts of the world.

The Menzels found four different types of this natural race: those like the shepherd, those like the dingo, those like the collie, and, especially in the south, those like the greyhound. With the exception of the herder dog, which is found only in the north, we can observe three other types with slight variations among the Himba. And among the pariah dogs in Africa we also find the typical stripe of the Rhodesian Ridgeback—a strip of fur on the back that grows against the rest of the fur.

Still, all dogs among the Himba are clearly of one kind, exactly as they were described by many past travelers to Africa and all dog scientists. Only one observation does not fit in with the old ones: negligence by humans. On the contrary, the dogs of the Himba are cared for and fed; they do not live at the edge of the settlement but right in the middle, along with the humans. They do not belong to an anonymous group but are individuals—each with its own name, as significant as the names of humans. They are valued and respected companions.

One night we were sitting with the town chief Wahenuna around a fire in

Like everywhere around the world, it is especially the children of the Himba who have a close relationship with the dogs. Metunai patiently lies beside some of her "protégés."

front of his hut; two of Wahenuna's dogs were lying between us. We were discussing our film project with Wahenuna and were trying to convince him that nothing bad would happen to his dogs in it. But at first we made a mistake.

The mistake consisted of a bag of Frolics. Everywhere on our travels we were able to use these dog treats to bribe our four-legged main characters. But Wahenuna reacted nervously: "What, do you want to poison my dogs?" Clearly this man had not had good experiences with white people. We calmly explained what the small brown pieces are made out of, that in the world that we come from they are used to feed dogs. Wahenuna remained skeptical.

Our only choice was to convince him with a demonstration. Slowly we started to eat a few Frolic pieces in front of him. This convinced the skeptic: after he, too, tried them, we were allowed to use them on Hakoquoko and Metunai—with the desired outcome. Soon the animals exhibited toward us the trustful and fearless behavior they usually reserve for the Himba of their kraal, and this was the most important precondition for filming.

A few kilometers north lay Kunene, the border river between Namibia and Angola. Up in the sky we could see the Southern Cross—and then we felt the familiar wet nose of a dog gently pushing against our hands in search of food.

The Canaan Dog

Aside from the special case of the basenji, only a small branch of the pariah and schensi dogs found from Africa to India's hinterlands has achieved racial honors in the eyes of the breeding federations of the industrialized nations: the Israeli Canaan dog. Professor Rudolfine Menzel, who, along with her husband Rudolf, did groundbreaking research on pariah dogs, in the 1930s discovered the pariahs of Palestine were useful for the military. She began controlled breeding, but the Canaan dog was only recognized by the International Purebred Dog Federation (FCI) as its own race shortly before Professor Menzel's death in 1973. The Canaan dog is the only race to emerge from the pariah dogs, a schensi dog that served humans as a herd dog in pre-Christian times.

The Canaan dog, which in some of its ancestral types closely resembles the dogs of the Himba, is considered to be intelligent and adaptable and is well regarded as a pet and guard dog. The Canaan dog shares all of these ancient characteristics with the other pariah dogs that live among the many peoples of tropical and subtropical areas and have remained nameless. The first club for the fans of this dog was founded in Germany in 1979.

The Rhodesian Ridgeback

The second representative of this race, who in genetic terms is also clearly a part of the dogs of the Himba, is the Rhodesian Ridgeback. Dogs with a strip of fur on their backbone that grows against the grain, the most noticeable physical characteristic of the Rhodesian Ridgeback, come from this dog's genetic pool. Rhodesian Ridgebacks were probably already highly regarded by Hottentot chiefs in Africa but only intentionally bred when white settlers crossbred the hunting dogs they had brought with them with the African animals. These dogs—almost seventy centimeters high, red-brown, grain-colored, or even lighter, sometimes with a black snout and ears—were used to deter lions and to guard or hunt slaves. The European and South African Rhodesian Ridgebacks are extremely quick and highly sensitive.

NEPAL

On the Tracks of the Holy Dogs

It is only because of the dog that the world exists.

From the Rig Veda, ca. 1200 b.c.

Suddenly we hear a light ringing of bells in the cold silence of the gorge. Then a second noise—the hoarse barking of big dogs. We soon see that we are coming upon a caravan of sheep and goats. Small brass bells tinkle on the red collars of the lead animals and the dogs.

The caravan is heading south toward one of the markets in the middle of Nepal. Wool and skins, semiprecious gems, and healing herbs are in the animals' bags; but salt is the main cargo, the white gold that "blossoms" as crystal foam on the shores of mineral lakes in Tibet. Only goats and sheep are fit "carriers" on the narrow mountain paths. Despite border controls by the Chinese, this tradition, which is over a thousand years old, continues.

"Namaste!" The caravan leader wished us good day as a greeting. The pack animals slowly continued along the border of the path, grazing on grass as they went. Two big, blue-black dogs shoved past us with mistrustful eyes. These dogs were once falsely called Tibetan mastiffs, but today they are referred to even in the West by their native name, do khyi. Today they are probably one of the rarest races in the world—and one of the oldest and most natural ones. Meeting them is like encountering a legend. Representations of them are on Babylonian clay tablets of the twelfth century b.c. The historian Herodotus reported that the satrap of Babylon kept a large pack of "Indian" dogs. A Chinese chronicle from 1121 b.c. tells of Ngao, the mastifflike dog of the emperor Wu Wang, a dog who was four-feet tall and was trained to fight all the emperor's enemies.

Similar reports from the classical period also exist: Greeks, Romans, and Persians owned these dogs from the eastern mountains. Alexander the Great is said to have taken a pair of these dogs, which he received as a gift from an Asian ruler, with him on the lion and elephant hunt. It was supposedly these dogs who had to fight with gladiators and kill wild bulls in the arenas of ancient Rome. Myths, legends, and secrets surround these big, strong animals who made it all the way to Europe from the highlands of Tibet, probably via China and India, at least two thousand years ago.

Historians tell us that do khyi were used as fighting and warrior dogs and were also precious assets of many rulers. But it is slowly becoming

Previous page: The magnificient Himalayas of Nepal, "residence of the gods."

clear that they also followed a different trail across Eurasia. Researchers found a remarkable similarity among the different peoples in the belt of Eurasian mountains from the Atlantic to the Hindu Kush: their dogs.

From Spain to Tibet the guard and farm dogs in the highlands, the mountains, and the valleys are all fairly similar, with only minor differences. They are big, heavy boned, and scraggly; they have ears that hang and—when they're excited—tails that curl above their backs. In Switzerland they are called Saint Bernards; in the French Pyrenees, Patou; across the border in Spain, Mastin de los Pireneos; in Portugal, Cao da Sera da Estrela; in Italy, Cane de Pastore Maremmano-Abruzzese; and in Anatolia, Akbash, Karabash, and Kangal. In Poland these dogs are known as Polski Owczarek; the Czechs call them Slovensky Cuvac; they are called Liptak in the Tatra mountains and in Romania; and in Hungary they guard the cattle under the name Kuvasz. A dog for many herder peoples and many different cultures; this animal helped all of them to survive in a wild and mostly hostile mountain world.

On its long journey this dog became what it is: a strong, stubborn, mistrustful guard concerned with the protection of humans and their property. The accounts by many researchers that described the dog as highly dangerous are not quite unfounded. The Venetian Marco Polo (1254–1324) gave the first description: "The people of Tibet are a bad-off race. They

For centuries sheep caravans have traveled the difficult mountain paths between Tibet and Nepal. Guarding them is the responsibility of the big do khyi. Alexander the Great is said to have owned a pair of these fearless animals.

keep mastiffs as big as donkeys that are suitable for the hunt of wild animals, especially the wild ox."

To this day little has changed in these evaluations. Author Peter Matthiessen expressed his fear of the do khyi, writing that the mastiffs are so vicious that Tibetan travelers wear an amulet on which is pictured a furious dog kept in chains.

It is therefore not suprising that at our first encounter with the do khyi we held our breath. But none of the animals attacked us; they merely reservedly observed us. After this experience, the well-meaning counsel of a do khyi researcher seemed amusing. He had advised us to always have a companion wearing local attire with us who would get along with the animals and they with him; to walk slowly and carry a stick, since in the case of an attack the dogs would first bite the stick; to never hit the dogs, since the noise of the wounded would call up all other dogs; and, if possible, to throw food to a threatening dog so that it would be occupied until we could reach safety.

We did not have to follow any of this advice: not once did these animals, who are so often described as being very aggressive, attack us. But they are always alert, independent protectors and guards with the herds and with their masters. Never threatening, they seem to create a calm zone through their confident and secure manner. They are true children of the mountains: reserved and mistrustful, and not everybody's friend.

The traders with their goat caravans value this as much as the nomadic herders with their yaks, whom we met later. Along a small river near their valley camp, the chained dogs erected a sort of off-limits area, a private area for the humans and a free area for the yaks and yak mixtures, inside of which the yaks could graze safely. Mixtures of yaks and cultured cattle, called dzoris, are very popular among the herder-farmers. Compared to the yaks, the dzo, the male dzoris, are softer and more easily directed. Dzomo, the cows, give more milk. To obtain animals with these desired qualities yaks and cattle have to be constantly crossed: their hybrids are as infertile as the products of crossbreeding between horses and donkeys.

These animals are the most valuable possessions of a family in the mountains of Nepal. And they require protection by the dogs. There are dangers everywhere on the way from the summer pastures in the mountains to the winter pen in the valley: leopards in the south of Nepal, very rare snow leopards in the north, and, of course, human attackers. As companions of the herds on their travels through many small hamlets, villages, cities, and settlements, the do khyi often leave their genetic mark among the local dog populations. The dogs on many small farms are strikingly reminiscent of the big Tibetan mastiffs, and yet they demonstrate the typical behavior of the pariah and schensi dogs around the world.

These local dogs are, especially in the middle and in the south of the country, the majority of the dogs we observed. They roam through settlements in packs, free and without a particular owner, nobody's enemy and everyone's friendly servant if there is even the most remote promise of food. They are real pariahs, animals living in packs alongside the human population.

But they are better off than their siblings farther south in the slums of India's big cities. Here in Nepal, whose inhabitants are shaped equally by Hinduism and Buddhism, the relationship of the many poor people to the even poorer animals is not one of cruel carelessness, not even in Kathmandu, the capital. We observed this during a five-day festival, in which on the second day dogs are honored with a special prayer celebration. This festival of dogs is called Kukur Tihar. A tika, the Hindu sign of luck, is painted on their foreheads with sandalwood paste—a third eye, which is considered to be the gate of enlightenment for humans

and animals. During Kukur Tihar the normally roaming pariahs are adorned with wreaths of flowers and spoiled with special delicacies offered to them on big platters. After all, they are considered to be the gatekeepers of Yama, the god of the dead, who decides whether the Hindu's next life will be a happy one or one of suffering.

We also experience this in Pashupatinah where Shiva, one of the three main gods of Hinduism, is honored in his incarnation as Pashupati, the master of animals. Along the shore of the Bagmati River, a huge temple city has grown around the Shiva altar, which is holy to the Nepalese. There

Raceless mixtures are not merely tolerated in Nepal, but accepted. Both Hinduism and Buddhism demand loving interaction with all living things. Buddhist prayer flags thus send thoughts of empathy around the world.

Travelers continue to report how dangerous the do khyi are. While it is true that because of their responsibility they are mistrustful of strangers, they are also faithful companions to their masters.

on the shore corpses are burned, the old body is given up, and the soul awaits a new, young body.

This body can be that of a dog, an insect, or a rat—depending on the karma of the dead, meaning his or her good or bad deeds, thoughts, and wishes. This belief of Hindus and Buddhists, who are already careful in their interactions with nature, also benefits the pariah dogs in the cities: each dog could be an ancestor on the path

On one day out of the year during the Kukur Tihar celebration, the dogs are the focus among Hindus. With flowers, wreaths, and the typical Hindu mark on the forehead the dogs are honored in the family as the guardians of the dead.

of change, or a close relative who passed away only recently. Thus the most aggression we saw directed toward the dogs was the throwing of a rock—aimed away from the dog—if the animal was too persistent.

The cynologist Ludwig Beckman's 1895 statement about all dogs of this type—from Africa to Asia to Latin America—surely applies to many of these pariahs in Kathmandu: they only arose out of "the wrecks of dog races of extinct cultural societies and mixed with the dogs of emigrating tribes and, in recent times, they mixed constantly with the introduced European dog races." (Indeed, even today one finds representatives of these "emigrated tribes," the grandchildren of the hippies and Europeans

According to Buddhist teaching, the souls of all living creatures are reincarnated after death in different bodies. Because dogs are especially close to humans, the soul of a human is often reincarnated into the body of a dog.

in search of enlightenment for whom Kathmandu, with its rich hashish supply in the 1970s, is still a mecca for the spiritual.) But we also saw pariahs as we otherwise only them saw in the north of Namibia. They are the same kind of dogs, with only minor differences in appearance, separated only geographically. For that reason they formed regional races.

We met the friendly pariahs of the streets of Kathmandu again during a small excursion to the temple of Swayambhunath, this time in idealized form: they were chiseled into stone as a semirelief. This sacred place, which because of the many rhesus monkeys that live here is also called the Monkey Temple, is one of the most important cultural centers of Buddhists as well as Hindus, even though it is overseen by Tibetan monks as a purely Buddhist place.

In front of the impressive stupa (a domelike hill overshadowed by a tower), the twelve Tibetan animals for the twelve months of the year are chiseled in stone 211 steps up. The dog is among them, since Buddha gave one month to it, too. The last year of the dog was 1994; 2006 will be the next, and it's already now eagerly anticipated. This is because a dog year is believed to be a time of good harvests, and among the twelve animals after which the years are named, the dog, along with the horse and the tiger, is considered to be the most favorable animal for humans. According to Buddhist belief, dogs are understanding, good-natured, faithful, and able, just as the humans born in the year of the dog are supposed to be.

This belief by no means refers exclusively to the do khyi and the pariahs, but also to the other group of dogs important to Buddhists, the lago khyi, the small, long-haired dogs from Tibet that have, just like their big relatives, found asylum in Nepal. Everywhere Buddhists live, the regard

The street dogs in Kathmandu profit from the Kukur Tihar celebration as well: humans aren't allowed to eat on this day until they have spoiled a dog with a feast.

The Kingdom of Nepal

Situated between China and India, at a length of nine hundred kilometers and a width of between 140 and 240 kilometers, from sea level to a height of up to 8848 meters, from tropical rain forests to snowy mountaintops, the independent kingdom Nepal (Niyampal, "the holy land") lies at the northern end of the Indian subcontinent. About eighteen million people, belonging to more than one hundred different ethnic groups, tribes, and peoples, live in this area between the Buddhist society in the north and the Hindu in the south.

There is little industry in Nepal, a cattle-farming, agrarian country focused mainly on local self-sufficiency. The country's biggest export is fertile earth: millions of tons of it are annually carried away to the Indian plains by the big streams that originate in the Himalayas. The land, once mostly covered by trees, has been deforested over the past fifty years as trees were used as firewood for the population and the constantly increasing number of trekking tourists and exported as building supplies. The monsoon rains carry away the shallow layer of topsoil of the now-bare earth and transport it into fast-flowing creeks, rivers, and streams that, like all the rivers in the country, end in the Ganges. This has led to a new problem: the rapidly growing population that needs more land for agriculture but loses it again and again to the rivers with each monsoon. Nepal has more erosion than almost any country on Earth. A program of reforestation has been launched to stop this ecological catastrophe.

Nepal owes its fame to its unique location in the Himalayas, a mountain range that attracts tourists from around the world. The majority of the highest mountains in the world are in the Himalayas, among them, on the border between China and Nepal, the most famous: Mount Everest. In the many religions in Nepal, the Himalayas (*himal* is Sanskrit and means "cradle of snow") represent the "residence of the gods."

For thousands of years almost all the important trading routes between China and India have led through Nepal, which as a result has developed not only close trade, but also a mixture of religions and cultures that makes this country one of the most fascinating cultural melting pots on Earth, one sustained by peacefulness and mutual respect.

It is said that the Buddha himself called all animals to him, but only twelve immediately followed his call. For this loyalty he gave each of the twelve, one of whom was the dog, one year in the Tibetan calendar. Humans born in the year of the dog are considered good-natured, trustworthy, and, above all else, faithful.

for them is high. This is because Buddhists believe that through these dogs a group of small lions that once played around the living Buddha continue to live. If there were a danger, the Buddha could immediately return these miniature animals to their full size, making them strong and powerful lions. Other legends also describe the Buddha's most faithful companions as small, lionlike dogs who could be turned into big, protective carnivores whenever there was a threat to their master. Eight of these strongly stylized mythical animals continue to carry the throne of the Dalai Lama, and they appear on Tibet's national flag, looking heroic.

For centuries they were not a separate race—but as "holy" dogs they were more or less purely bred, always with the goal of making them resemble a small lion. Because the dogs were bred in different areas and according to the different aesthetic preferences of their owners—who live predominantly in monasteries—different types developed. These differ-

The legend of the holy dogs goes back to a myth according to which the Buddha was always surrounded by a group of small lions who in the case of danger could instantly grow to their full size. Dogs have been bred to resemble the Buddha's most faithful companions.

ent types became the ancestors of all the lapdogs who in the West are considered descendants of the holy dogs of Tibet.

Today, far from Tibet, five races claim to be descendants of the holy dogs of monks: the Lhasa apso, the shih tzu, the Pekinese, the Tibetan terrier, and the Tibetan spaniel. They probably all owe their existence to

the various forms of the lago khyi, a small dog. The racial differences we see today probably appeared very early, since the dogs of Tibet had access to the Chinese emperor court, where stylized and miniaturized depictions of nature, similar to the Bonsai art that was later developed in Japan, were considered signs of nobility.

These small creatures were mentioned in Chinese literature from 500 B.C. A little later the ha pa was mentioned, a dog who spent its time below the low tables of the wealthy Chinese. In the seventeenth century a dog called tschin mao shih tzu, a golden lion-dog appeared in an emperor's dictionary. Marco Polo mentioned a similar animal in Venice four centuries earlier upon his return from the Far East.

The do khyi are considered an important part of Tibetan culture. Even the Dalai Lama, until he was exiled, kept some of these beautiful dogs. For the young monks in this monastery in Kathmandu, Sambho is a wonderful playmate.

These dogs were only introduced in the West by explorers, travelers, and British colonial officers as shih tzu khyi and apso. *Shih tzu khyi* simply means "dogs of Tibetan kind," and *apso* merely signifies a special characteristic of the animals, the "hairy mustache." Significant differences seem not to have existed between them originally.

In Tibet, and in the Buddhist monasteries in India and Nepal where Tibetans found asylum, these dogs are by no means as standardized as they are in the West through controlled breeding. We met Lhasa apsos who could also have been Tibetan terriers and shih tzus who only differed from Pekinese, with their typical small faces, by their slightly longer noses.

Jay Singh, former president of the dog club of Nepal and thoroughly knowledgeable about all races in the Himalayan area, had already drawn our attention to the fact that the Western nomenclatures had little significance among the dwarf dogs of his home. He also told us that the increasing interest in lapdogs among Western buyers has led to a strong increase in the breeding of apsos, shih tzus, terriers, spaniels, and Pekinese, especially in Kathmandu. All of them were certainly purebred, but in the sense that they traced back to ancestors in one of the many Buddhist monasteries and were all considered holy dogs because they are supposed to resemble Buddha's lions. But their value in the eyes of Western buyers only derives from their originating from Nepal, a country full of myths and legends.

The breeding of these races, which began in England and is now practiced throughout the West, is only valuable (in spite of Westerners' questionable belief in sharply delineated races) because these dogs are extremely threatened in what is believed to be their home, Tibet. This applies especially to the large do khyi. The Chinese, who occupied Tibet in 1959, quickly recognized these native animals, who protected homes and herds to be a decisive pillar in the Tibetan farmer and nomad culture, firmly anchored in their traditions and religion. Even the Dalai Lama—the god ruler in the Potala Palace in Lhasa until 1959 when he was exiled—had some of these large guard dogs in his summer garden. A collar made of dyed yak hair emphasized the lion head of his animals.

The Chinese opened the hunt on the dogs. At first a general directive from the head of state and party, Mao Tse-tung, ordered all useless eaters to be destroyed. Every singing bird one can think of whom the state suspected of stealing grain was a victim of this persecution, as well as dogs and cats. An increase in rats and mice, and damaging

The Tibetan

A fascinating mixture of different peoples and ethnic groups has shaped Nepal, and tolerance and good neighboring have a long tradition here. In spite of its poverty, Nepal is open to refugees who do not find tolerance at home.

One of the best-known Tibetan population groups are the Sherpa, who came to Nepal, more than five hundred years ago. They make their home in the high mountains and are famous for being good guides on mountain expeditions. This has led to the false impression that *Sherpa* is synonymous with "mountain guide." *Sherpa* actually means "people from the east" and signifies their original homeland in eastern Tibet.

With the violent annexation of Tibet by the Chinese in 1959, a massive flow of refugees began hemorrhage. According to estimates, about one hundred thousand Tibetans have left their homeland since the Chinese invasion. Many followed the Dalai Lama, the spiritual and worldly leader of the Tibetans who escaped to India at the beginning of the occupation. To this day and under continuing pressure to assimilate, entire families and villages flee to Nepal where their religion and way of life are respected and where Tibetan refugees enjoy asylum status. It is believed there are roughly fifteen thousand Tibetan refugees in Nepal.

These people, who consist half of sedentary farmers and half of farming nomads, have little difficulty adjusting to life here, especially among the Buddhists who constitute the majority in northern Nepal. Used to the hard life in the mountains, the immigrants find an environment that is very much like their original home.

Their animals are brought along, especially yaks and yak hybrids, goats and sheep, on rare occasions horses, and the necessary guard dogs for the cattle. An effective border control is hardly possible in the high mountains. That is why trade caravans from Tibet continue to reach Nepal; the Tibetans are traditionally considered good traders. Their main trade is in the salt that is needed to prepare butter tea, the national drink of both countries.

insects on the fields was the consequence. Only after Mao's death in 1976 did the persecution in China start to ebb. Although in Tibet it was continued in an effort to enhance Chinese hegemony by destroying traditional Tibetan structures.

Their first victim other than the humans was the "inheritance of the Himalayas," as Jay Singh calls the do khyi, who are now threatened by extinction. He has worked for more than twenty years on their stock. Singh grew up with them; his father, who was once the raja of Tholara, kept the Tibetan dogs as a status symbol and for protection of the palace.

Today five races can be traced back to the lion-dogs: Lhasa apsos, shih tzus, Pekinese, Tibetan terriers, and Tibetan spaniels. However, this strict differentiation among races is made by Western breeders and is unknown in the dog's homelands.

The dogs are also threatened by increasing traffic and tourism in their asylum country Nepal, as well as by changes in the way of life of the different peoples. Where once the inaccessibility of mountain territory allowed clearly definable races to develop and remain stable, humans and their animals now pass through, and the result is increasingly mixed pariah packs.

But we learned to love these as well, especially at the small airport of Nepalganj in the southwest where we returned in our small Twin Otter after an expedition to the north. Wagging their tails and full of joy at our return, the dogs greeted us at the plane's steps. We had met them earlier when a few weeks before we waited at the airport for our departure. Giving them a few treats at our first meeting was all they needed to become our friends.

They stood there like a big family welcoming a long-lost member back into their circle. This moving reception in a foreign place made us love these pariahs as much as the powerful do khyi or the wispy apsos in the mountains and monasteries. We now had a much better understanding of the Buddhist saying that accompanied us in our thoughts throughout this trip: "The interaction with a dog is beneficial for humans."

The Lhasa Apso

It wasn't until 1921 that the first of these dogs, favorites of the religious elite in ancient Tibet, arrived in Europe and the United States. Because of the Lhasa apso's dignified appearance, balanced temper, and enormous courage, the race quickly became popular. Since 1934 it has been recognized by the International Purebred Dog Federation (FCI) and categorized as a community and companion dog. The Lhasa apso is about twenty-eight centimeters tall and weighs up to seven kilograms. It has a distinctive shape to its head, which is covered by the long, heavy fur that drapes around the rest of its body. The tail is carried above the back and is also covered by fur. The Lhasa apso is bred in the colors gold, sand, gray, and black, as well as in many shades between black and gold. Lhasa apsos can also be tricolored.

As a member of the family, the Lhasa apso is faithful, close, and cuddly, but it is also always alert and ready to bark at the unknown. It is as reserved toward strangers as the other lion-dogs. The dog's fur needs to be brushed daily. Training is easy.

The term Lhasa apso is not used in the dog's native countries. *Apso* refers to all small long-haired dogs whose evolution traces back to the legend of Buddha's lions. Only Western breeders started separating the different types, which probably evolved out of local differences among the widely separated monasteries, into different races. Tibetan spaniels, Tibetan terriers, shih tzus, and Pekinese probably all trace back to the original monastery dogs.

The Do Khyi

At the beginning of this century Englishmen brought some of these big, heavy dogs to Great Britain to breed, calling them Tibetan mastiffs. They are recognized by the FCI as representatives of guard and herd dogs under the general category of mountain dogs.

The do khyi is an impressive dog with a height of at least sixty-five centimeters and a weight of up to eigthy-two kilograms. It has a broad, massive head, heavy hindquarters, and well-formed ribs in a broad chest. The dog's straight hair is short in the face but long and thick elsewhere. Despite its thickness, it does not get matted and requires little care. The dog's recognized colors are black, golden brown, and gray.

The do khyi still demonstrates all its original characteristics. While it is a calm, confident dog, it has a well-formed guarding instinct and remains reserved and mistrustful of strangers. In the family it is good-natured, but also stubborn and independent. For this reason do khyi only belong with people who know them well and can patiently train them.

MOROCCO

Kitmir's Heirs

His master is like a servant to him. At night he rests beside his dog and prepares him his own place, so that during the day he walks beside him as a proud warrior.

Hasan Abu Nuwas,

court poet of Harun ar Raschid, Baghdad, ca. 790 b.c.

Sand-colored, long-legged, arrogant: like the three kings were stepping up to Jesus, this sloughi trio walks at their master's side among the spectators, who step back to let them pass. The dogs see everybody and everything, but they do not seem to be looking at anybody or anything. Unmoved, they grant humans only the gift of their presence.

The dogs exhibit this aloof attitude even though this is their celebration, which takes place once a year here in the hills of the Atlas Mountains in southwestern Morocco, bringing together humans and dogs from all over the kingdom. Mohammed and Mokhtar, for example, traveled over five hundred kilometers in a rental car from Marrakech; they brought with them food, dates, water, and their sloughis.

Mohammed and Mokhtar pull into the village square of Imin Tatelt, the small *douar*, or Moroccan village, where hunters and hunting dogs meet. It is a holy place, dedicated to Marabout Yakoub, the wise man and scribe. Its inhabitants call themselves Ben Yakoub, "sons of Jacob," and many also apply this name to this picturesque settlement that lies between two mountain slopes and is turned into a fair for three days a year.

This is a fair of faithfulness and vanities. The hunters arrive singing and praying. In contrast to their dogs, they enjoy the attention that the elegant animals receive. The Ben Yakoub stand next to one another happily and enthusiastically, even though they know more about the annual celebration than most other Moroccans.

Previous page: The aidis' scraggly fur protects them against injuries—not only in fights with other aidis, but also in fights with other animals. They are scheduled to be recognized soon as their own race; until recently they were often insultingly called herder hybrids.

"It is still always something special to see these wonderful animals so close up," says a water salesman who, in his enthusiasm, gives free refreshments to the children. He can afford it, since he and his neighbors will get a portion of the compensation the village receives in food each time it hosts hunters and pilgrims.

The visitors brought fourteen cattle with them this year. According to Muslim rituals the cattle are slaughtered in the village square. The meat then goes to the hosts. This compensation is a good reason to continue celebrating the wise Marabout who is said to still work miracles on occa-

sion, even centuries after his death, as are the donations that many pilgrims leave at his grave.

Marabout seems to have worked a small but important miracle this time as well: the sloughi hunters this year remain undisturbed in Imin Tatelt. The feared gamekeeper from the provincial capital Tata did not appear. The gamekeeper could confiscate the dogs: hunting with the quick sloughis has been prohibited in this area for a long time.

This is why invitations to such events are made secretively and why at times they are abruptly postponed, as happened the previous year. We are proud to be able to document this century-old tradition. It is nice that the gamekeeper shied away from making the exhausting trek through the mountains. Maybe the prayers of one of the hunters brought about this small miracle—Jacob looking out for his sons!

And in doing this he also cares for the sloughis, because this meeting is incredibly important for the continuation of the race and the pureness and quality of the offspring. This festival has the significance of the large dog shows in Europe. Mokhtar tell us, "If I see that someone here has a better dog than myself, I try to return the next year with an even better one." The celebration of the Ben Yakoub is thus also a sort of natural show

Every year in one of the remote villages in the Anti Atlas, the sloughi hunters of Morocco meet. For three days there are religious slaughters, ceremonies, and hunts with the noble dogs to honor a deceased holy person.

that continually tests, compares, and improves the standard for this race.

The actual climax of the event offers an opportunity for this as well: after the conclusion of the religious celebration the hunt begins—the big social event for the sloughi owners. This time there are more than forty dogs on the hunt through the semidesert, the rocky, thorny steppe, and the lunar landscape of the sand dunes that glow in an array of colors. Of course it is a different hunt from the one the rich Berber barons once held here. In 1912 the sloughi lover August le Gras described the spectacle in the *German Greyhound-Breeding Book* like this:

Before important occasions the sloughis are painted with henna. Symbols such as the hand of Fātimah, the daughter of the prophet Muhammad, are supposed to protect the valuable dog from the "evil eye" of jealous neighbors.

> The sloughis are placed on horses and the rider holds them with his left arm, while the right hand holds the reins. Then a herd of gazelles, still fairly far away, comes into sight. Forward now, ventre à terre.
>
> The riders crouch over the necks of their horses, the Arab cloaks are blowing behind, clouds of sands rise. Then the gazelles spot their archenemies, the humans. They run. Now the sloughi starts his work. The rider encourages him, lets him go. The sloughi jumps to the ground, completely fresh, and like the wind goes after the gazelles, camouflaged by his sand color.
>
> Sloughi and the ground are one, until the gazelle spots the new enemy, unfortunately too late. Just a few jumps and it is over: the fine and tender animal is strangled. The sloughi now waits until his master arrives and rewards his quickness and joy of hunting.

Today, almost a century later, this is unfortunately only a memory: there is no more hunt by horse and no gazelles in the big country. But one thing, expressed by August le Gras in the following passage, is the same: "It is beautiful to see the Sloughi in the field, see his huge leaps, how excited he is, how his eyes are glowing. And what endurance, what lungs.

He never breathes heavily, is always fresh, courageous, and inexhaustible."

This is how we experienced these dogs as well—albeit without gazelles, and with only a few rabbits as prey, but still with the same joy, with almost Olympian enthusiasm. The goal is not victory or the prey, but participation and enjoying the moment. Even with the gamekeeper threatening, this festival is the only way for the sloughis and their masters to keep alive the ancient inheritance, their lifestyle, their culture, and their tradition.

In North Africa, the Near East, and the Far East, from Persia via the Arabic peninsula to the Atlantic, thin, fast hunting dogs coud be found in ancient times; indeed, they are pictured on the pharaoh graves of ancient Egypt. Only a few recognized races were able to develop out of this: the saluki in the east, the sloughi in Morocco and Tunisia, and the azawakh in Mali, Niger, Burkina Faso, and Chad.

Although these dogs are bred and used differently in the various regions, they are all related. Possibly the greyhoundlike pariahs who lived with humans ten thousand years ago in the Far East are their ancestors; maybe the Gaelic greyhounds who were brought by the Romans to North Africa influenced the appearance of today's dogs. Regardless, it is clear that they are the result of a very special bond between human and animal, a bond that could only have been formed on the hunt through the hot sand of the desert.

Even Islam, which otherwise counts dogs among the impure animals, validates this bond. The eighteenth sura of the Koran recounts the story of the seven sleepers who were prosecuted because of their beliefs and who found refuge in a mountain cave. One of them had Kitmir along, his favorite dog. The men were afraid that Kitmir would bark and betray their location, so they tried to drive the animal away. But Allah gave Kitmir the power of speech and the dog said, "I love all those who are important to God. So go to sleep; I will watch over you." Kitmir kept his promise for

The holy book of Islam reports that a dog once protected seven young men who were persecuted because of their beliefs. In thanks, when it died, the dog, Kitmir, was allowed entry into paradise by Muhammad.

In the small douars the tradition of sloughi breeding has been kept alive to this day. Yet Mohammed and Mokhtar were hesitant to show us their dogs. The memory is too fresh of the French colonial powers who were so fascinated by the beauty of the dogs that they stole them.

Morocco

Morocco lies in northwestern Africa and is separated from Europe by only the Strait of Gibraltar, which is thirteen kilometers wide. About twenty-six million people live in the country, which, with an area of 710,850 square kilometers (including the part of the western Sahara occupied by Morocco), is about twice the size of Germany.

In 1956 Morocco gained independence from Spain and France. Since then the country has been a constitutional, democratic, social monarchy. King Hassan II unites worldly as well as spiritual power in Morocco. Each year on the anniversary of his inauguration the leading Islamic religious men, leaders of parties, and other persons of honor take an oath of faithfulness and obedience to the king for the entire population.

Morocco's main tourist attraction is its variety of terrain: ocean and desert border mountain regions; old feudal cities lie among isolated mountain villages. Three mountain chains of the Atlas cut through the country from the southwest to the northeast: the Middle Atlas, which are up to 3,440 meters high and about four hundred kilometers long; the High Atlas, which are over four thousand meters high and eight hundred kilometers long; and the Anti-Atlas which are up to twenty-five hundred meters high and three hundred kilometers long. North of the mountains lie fertile plains; south of them the Sahara begins, with steppelike semideserts interspersed with chains of oases.

309 years, until the seven were found and Kitmir allowed them to wake up. As thanks for its faithfulness, the animal was granted entrance to paradise after its death.

Even though the sura makes no reference to Kitmir's race, the legend portrays the dog as a sloughi, just as it portrayed the animal belonging to the prophet Muhammad. Aside from their hunting abilities it is this myth about Kitmir that explains why the noble greyhounds, Kitmir's heirs, enjoy such a high regard in the Far East, a special position among all dog races.

The French general and hippologist Daumas described this vividly in his 1853 book, *The Horses of the Sahara:*

> Here, as in all other Arab countries, the dog is no more than a neglected, annoying servant who is pushed away regardless of its usefulness, regardless of whether he is guarding the homestead or the cattle. Only the greyhound enjoys the affection, the respect, and the tenderness of its master. Rich and poor alike regard him as the necessary companion of all noble joys, which the Bedouins practice with such joy. One guards this dog like one's own child, one gives him special food, allows him to share a plate with oneself, so to speak, and very carefully watches over the purity of the race. A man of the Sahara does not mind traveling twenty or thirty miles to find a noble male for his noble female.

Today an owner may travel up to several hundred miles for the sloughis, as we observed in the village of Jacob's sons. The breeding of sloughis, which was once spread throughout the Maghreb states, has suffered many setbacks, in part because of the loss of power of provincial lords and nobles in the kingdom of Morocco.

Once a French and Portuguese protectorate, Morocco gained independence in 1956. One of the first resolutions of Sultan Mohammed V, who assumed the title of king in 1957, was to destroy the country's rich and mighty sheiks. The sheiks lost tax privileges and land, along with, and because of the resulting loss in income, the means to keep up their huge dog kennels. Some of these kennels housed over two hundred purebred hunting sloughis.

The vast expanses at the edge of the Sahara are home to the sloughis. Here, over generations, the dogs developed their endurance and running ability.

The consequences this had for dog breeding are comparable to the consequences of the October Revolution in Russia in 1917. Then too the dog breeding practiced by the aristocracy almost died out. The Borzoi, Russia's greyhound, was kept alive for the dog world only because of the initiative of a few emigrants and enthusiasts abroad. But regardless of how careful the selection and how much love, caring, and knowledge were given, the conditions of the Russian homeland could not be replaced, and the working animals of the steppe turned into idle street dogs.

This fate also could have befallen the sloughis in Morocco had it not been for a few active friends of the race who enabled the animals to survive in their country. "Threatened in its existence" is how in 1968 Pierre Durel referred to the sloughi, who at first lost its breeding home through the courts, and through the prohibition of the hunt almost everywhere also lost its function. Bitterly, Durel concluded that "not the hunt with the sloughi, but the sloughi itself" had been pronounced illegal.

The sloughi was saved by people like Durel—Europeans who advocated for this ancient race. Among them was the now deceased Italian princess Ruspoli who immigrated to Morocco. Her sloughis—she kept up

With the demise of the once mighty sheik, the sloughi breeding was threatened. But the powerful love of simple men for this dog allowed it to survive. Today Morocco once again proudly acknowledges the heritage of these desert dogs and is setting the standards for this breed.

to sixty animals in her palace and large gardens—were comparable to the breeds kept by some of the sheiks in the past. For example, at the sloughi kennel kept in the 1930s by the uncle of the then reigning sultan at Safi, south of Casablanca, an army of servants cared for a pack of about sixty to seventy grown animals and forty to fifty puppies; and in the stables were kept about fifteen horses with whom the dogs were trained for the hunt.

The sheiks' favorite dogs accompanied their masters to receptions where they rested on their own cushions. To exhibit their nobility silver medals bearing their family tree were hung around their necks. Sloughis who had made a name for themselves by hunting boar proudly displayed the images of a few boar on their collars.

Expropriation, hunting laws, the increasing cultivation of former hunting grounds, industrialization, and the growing influence of Western civilization have fundamentally changed the lives of humans and dogs. Game has almost disappeared; only the hunt for rabbits, fennecs, and jackals are left. But, to their surprise, the friends of the sloughi began to reverse the negative trend in the 1970s.

The Europeans—by far not as wealthy as the Italian princess, but just like her active fans of these beautiful animals—were the first to have an effect. Then followed the Moroccans, who did not want to abandon the traditional dog of their homeland. They all keep sloughis mostly in urban or suburban conditions: running grounds have replaced the open field for their dogs.

Increasingly sloughis are found in the provinces again, among farmers and herders who use their animals for the jackal hunt, just like once upon a time the Borzoi in Russia hunted wolves. In 1992 Ingeborg and Eckhart E. Schritt described the situation in the countryside like this: "The farther away from the accomplishments and disturbances of civilization, the better are the conditions for the sloughi and its undisturbed life according to ancient tradition. There is simply a strong relationship between the people and the race that not even government hunting laws can destroy."

And that does not allow itself to be destroyed, as our visit in Imin Tatelt proved. The enthusiasm of some and the stubbornness of others would not have been enough alone to save the sloughi from extinction. Pride had to be added: Morocco is the only North African country to join the International Pure-Bred Federation (FCI), and since 1973 it has decided on the standard of the race. Today a Moroccan sloughi club oversees the adherence to these standards.

Morocco's King Hassan supports using the animal again in its ancient role; after all, sloughis are considered to be the national race. Aside from keeping a pack of the finest dogs, the king also owns private hunting grounds, complete with gazelles. Of course, hunting with sloughis is allowed for the king only, not the average citizens. But the citizens do it nonetheless. We witnessed this among the Ben Yakoub and farther north in the country.

Up north we also met dogs known as the chin. *Chin* in Arabic refers to a dog considered impure by the religious Muslim. The chin suffers through life the way Daumas described it in 1853—and worse. A chin is a pariah dog, a stray village dog, or sometimes a dog kept in the yard. Mohammed, like most farm owners, keeps a few of them on his farm on the plateau between Safi and Marrakech. They are not fed; the animals have to look for their own food, often in the garbage. In contrast the sloughis—who are never simply referred to as "dogs"—receive a nutritious mix of olive oil and flour.

One is fed because it is pure; the other is not pure because it is not fed—an absurd consequence of ancient hygiene customs. But worse was what we found on the side of the road as we left Mohammed's village. There, unattended, lay the unwanted puppies, killed with a stone. The dogs died because they were impure and worthless. This fate would be unthinkable for sloughi puppies: if their owner did not want to keep them,

The Berber

The ancient Greeks viewed themselves as an educated and cultured people. All others, who "stammered" unintelligibly were called *barbaroi*. Why this term stuck only for the original inhabitants of North Africa is not clear.

The different Berber tribes never considered themselves to be related and at most had changing alliances with one another. When in the seventh century Arabs began to conquer Morocco, the Berbers were pushed back into the mountain and rural areas. The Berbers are most closely associated with the nomads of this region.

Today, the language of the Berber is spoken only in the Er Rif, a mountain range in the High and Middle Atlas. In the cities and settlements that were among the first to fall under Arab influence the language of the colonizers, especially of the Bedouins in the east, prevailed. This is partly because Arabic, unlike the Berber language, has a written component.

Also belonging to the Berber tribes spread throughout Algeria, Libya, and Chad are the nomad Bedouins of the Sahara and the Sahel— the Tuareg, whose azawakhs are similar to the hunting dogs of their sedentary or nomadic cousins in the north. The original Berber culture that until the early Middle Ages was shaped by the late Stone Age is today mostly assimilated into the North African cultural melting pot. It has only remained pure in some isolated areas, especially in the social and political structures of villages, the right to marry, and the role of women. Women are given greater freedom among the Berber than among the Arabs. Berber women, for example, do not have to wear a veil and often know how to read and write.

it would be easy to sell them, in many cases for a lot of money.

We drove on, heading south, away from sloughi country and into the High Atlas Mountains. Morocco boasts deserts, rough mountains, palm trees, and snows—an incredible multiplicity of landscapes and people. Here in the rising mountains we met Berber nomads who, along with sedentary Berbers, are Morocco's original inhabitants.

Only sparse grass, bushes, and herbs grow here among the boulders and rocky undergrowth of the mountain slopes. But this is sufficient for the nomads' sheep and goat herds, who are accompanied by robust, long-haired herder dogs. These dogs are called aidis. They are the other significant type of dog in Morocco, a sort of counter-model to the sloughi.

The aidi is only found in Morocco; it looks different only a few mountains to the east. And yet this dog is like an old acquaintance: in Nepal we met its Asian cousin the do khyi. In Morocco the working dog has developed into the aidi, a living inheritance from the Stone Age of all peoples.

One can find the working dog around the Mediterranean Sea; in the mountain ranges across central and eastern Europe; across Asia Minor; from the Caucasus across the Himalayas up to the China Sea. Probably coming from the East, warriors and traders have taken the animals with them halfway around the world. And wherever they settled a new "race" of working dog developed, only slightly differing from its ancestors.

In contrast to the sloughis the aidi was not carefully bred either; the only selection was natural. Sick aidis are not nursed, weak ones are not cured, and puppies are not taken care of in a special manner: what cannot live will die. This is a brutal logic, but it guarantees a healthy race, hardy in unfriendly environments that only enable the most fit to survive.

Researchers group the aidi in the category of farmer, guard, and herder dogs. The dogs in this category might have been used as war dogs in earlier times, which would explain why they always originate around bases and other military facilities. It also would explain the open mistrust and at times aggressive behavior they exhibit toward most strangers.

Working dogs serve only the herders, who can only live their traditional lives with the help of dogs. Like the dogs related to them the aidis do not guide the herds but merely guard them. In this function they do not simply react aggressively but actually differentiate between harmless hikers and thieves. They also pursue wolves and jackals without mercy.

Dogs who protect like the aidis, are the most ancient companions of herds. Their mostly smaller and more agile relatives, the herder dogs, evolved much later. Eventually well-rounded animals like the German shepherd, combined the abilities to both protect and guide the herds. But up in the High Atlas the dogs are still entirely directed toward protection and defense. The guarding instinct is inborn, while the defense function came through the strong selection pressure that animal and human enemies exert: only strong animals survive attacks.

The aidis carry out both functions to perfection. Each aidi knows its

The dogs of the Berber nomads certainly are not as noble as the sloughis, but they are well adapted to the natural conditions and the needs of their owners. Aidis not only protect the cattle but also secure the campsites against unwanted guests—be they human or animal.

own sheep and goats, and they in turn know their aidi. The aidis supervise the herds perfectly, protect them on moves, and when the herd is grazing spreads the animals out to strategic places so as to be able to drive away a hostile stranger. This shows the quality of the race: humans do not have to give this dog any orders. A combination of alertness, understanding, and initiative allows the aidi to handle even very complex procedures.

On the summer grazing grounds of a nomad family we met some especially beautiful examples of this race: three big, long-haired dogs who perfectly fit the provisional standard that has developed for the aidi. The dogs must appear strong, mighty, and muscular, with a low rib cage and a mane around the neck

Moroccans clearly differentiate between the noble sloughis and the raceless mixtures. Even though as guard dogs they often perform useful tasks such chins are considered less worthy. Unlike the sloughis they are not fed, and they therefore have to live off leftovers and garbage.

and throat. Most important, the aidi's fur should resemble a shield that protects it in fights against animals and the weather.

The three dogs from the High Atlas exhibited these characteristics and many more that have more of an aesthetic than performance value— for example, dry lips with black or brown contours, always in accord with the nose and the color of the fur. Not all aidis we met had these; the nomad dogs mix all too easily with the pariahs from the villages.

Until recently the aidi was branded a herder hybrid but it is scheduled to be recognized as another Moroccan dog race soon. This dog definitely does not belong in a city apartment. The habitat and way of life of these animals are too closely connected. Although aidis are not noble luxury animals, they are like the sloughi in their ability to work hard in a harsh environment.

A life as a pet would rob both these animals of a defining part of their identity. This is how the Borzoi and some terriers lost part of their character. The moral of an anecdote told by Hans Jörgen Strassner, azawakh friend and traveler in Africa, applies to all of them. According to the anecdote, in 1853 the Egyptian vice-regent, Abba Pascha, said to the messenger of King Wilhelm I. von Württemberg, Freiherr on Hügel: "I do not doubt that you will be able to obtain Arab horses. But do not believe that you will now be able to breed Arabs; because each pure-blooded Arab is only pure-blooded as long as it breathes the expanse of the desert and feels its warmth under its hooves."

What applies to the desert horses of Africa is also valid for the dogs from these regions. On our Morocco trip we grew to be friends with the sloughi and the aidi. And we doubt that these races could remain true to themselves far away from their homes. Two of their most important abilities would be rendered useless and eventually lost: their adherence to those instincts advantageous for humans, and their adaptation to human needs in an often unforgiving environment. We hope that the freedom of humans and dogs remains possible in Morocco for a long time to come.

Hunting with the sloughi is illegal today in most parts of Morocco. A French expert even worried about the extinction of the sloughis. Happily, his prediction did not come true.

The Sloughi

The European enthusiasm for North African greyhounds started in the nineteenth century and led to relatively early breeding attempts outside of the Maghreb, this despite the fact that around the turn of the century the German world-traveling hunter Max Siber declared sloughis to be "dumb animals, without a nose, without the ability to search, without loyalty and without obedience." In 1907 the first sloughis arrived in England but were not yet differentiated racially from their cousins, the salukis, a differentiation that is also foreign to many Arabs. But the FCI makes a clear distinction: salukis always have medium length to long fur, while sloughis always have short straight fur.

The Swiss cynologist Hans Räber believes the differences among Arabic dog races are "very fluid." For example, there are breeding families that contain dogs with longer fur as well as dogs with short, straight fur. The azawakh, who used to be thought of as a perversion of the sloughi, is now also listed as an independent race.

Sloughis are long-distance runners, in contrast to sprinters like the whippet or greyhound. On longer runs they can reach speeds between fifty and fifty-five kilometers per hour. The preferred color of their fur is light red or sand colored. Solid black or white dogs are undesirable. According to Räber different local kinds of sloughis exist in Maghreb who deviate from the standard that is bred in Europe and Morocco.